A Year of Romance

Twelve Months

of Romantic

Ideas to

Light Up

Your Love Life

MARA GOODMAN-DAVIES

SOURCEBOOKS CASABLANCA™
AN IMPRINT OF SOURCEBOOKS, INC.®
NAPERVILLE, ILLINOIS

Published by Sourcebooks, Inc.
P.O. Box 4410, Naperville, Illinois 60567-4410
(630) 961-3900
FAX: (630) 961-2168
www.sourcebooks.com

 Library of Congress Cataloging-in-Publication Data

Goodman-Davies, Mara.
 A year of romance : Twelve months of romantic ideas to light up your love
life / by Mara Goodman-Davies.
     p. cm.
 ISBN 1-5707-1999-3 (pbk.)
 1. Man-woman relationships—Miscellanea. 2. Couples—Recreation. I.
Title.
 HQ801 .G5916 2002
 306.7—dc21

                                                          2002010516

Printed and bound in the United States of America
VHG 10 9 8 7 6 5 4 3 2 1

This book is dedicated to my husband, Justin Davies,
my very own "Prince of Wales"

Acknowledgments

I would like to thank my agent Gareth Esersky for her endless support and belief in me; Deborah Werksman of Sourcebooks, for being a brilliant and fearless editor; my husband Justin for teaching me about true romance; Judith Kelly of Sourcebooks for working with me on PR; my best friend Katelyn for eighteen years of friendship, support, and "second sight"; my mom Roni for expert financial advice and my inherited "you can do it" attitude; Maria Cassidy for years of good friendship; Thomas Cook and Thomas Jacowski for being the brothers I never had; and Mary Francis Turner for being my maid of honor.

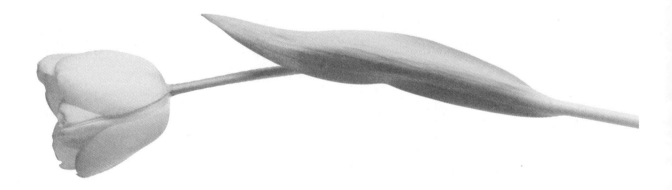

Contents

Spring

HAVE A SPRING FLING

When spring pops its lovely little head up from a long winter's nap, it is also time for love to come into full bloom! Spring is a time of rebirth and renewal. Catch yourself a good case of "spring fever" as you enter the most romantic season of the year.

MONDAY–FRIDAY AROMATHERAPY

Sunday

Relaxation: Vetiver

Vetiver is most effective as a calming, quieting agent. It will help you feel more grounded and solid in your relationship.

Monday

Clarity: Orange Blossom

Orange blossom can lift your spirits and calm your deepest fears, making even the biggest emotional mountain feel like a molehill.

Tuesday

Balance: Angelica

Angelica helps you achieve physical, spiritual, and emotional alignment. Promotes wholeness, individually and as a couple.

Wednesday

Healing: Carrot Seed

Carrot seed is a body purifier and will help you get rid of anything that's toxic to your system, restoring you to your healthy, sexy self!

Thursday

Rejuvenation: Orange Leaves

An orange leaf bath will leave you feeling alert, cleansed, and refreshed.

Friday

Passion: Ylang Ylang

Ylang Ylang helps you rekindle those infatuated, flirtatious feelings of new love, and promotes a healthy fantasy break from daily routines.

Saturday

Play: Grapefruit

Grapefruit makes you sharp, witty, and ready for anything. After a grapefruit massage, you and your lover will feel spry, agile, and bursting with energy.

SPRING ACTIVITIES

Milk a Cow

Don't laugh! This can be a very romantic process, especially for you city slickers. Why? Because this is an outdoor activity that you and your lover would probably NEVER do (unless you both live on farms.) Since milking a cow will be a new adventure for the two of you, the sense of wonder and surprise that you will go through when you grab onto those udders for the first time will be absolutely exhilarating. This is great for your relationship because you are learning and discovering a new activity together. The fact that the two of you are willing to do something like this shows great versatility, adaptability, and a willingness to "stretch" your boundaries. To find a willing cow, just call a milk or dairy farm in your area and tell them what you want to do. If you live in a big city, check the surrounding countryside. You may have to travel a little, but the anticipation will make it worth the trip. Don't forget to bring your camera (or videotape it to share with friends and have a good laugh later). This back-to-basics romantic experience is sure to MOOOOOOve your relationship to a deeper level.

Mow the Lawn

If the farm life is just not for you, then you and your lover can still have a wonderful time tending to your own yard. A menial task like mowing the lawn can become romantic when you do it as a team. If you think about it, there is something very sweet about cutting the first grass of the spring season together. You are partaking in a ritual that signifies the season of renewal.

Play by a Babbling Brook

You and your lover can rediscover your childlike sense of innocence as you skip stones and follow the running water until you find its end. If you live near a wooded area, have a great time rambling through the trees. If you live in a city, go to a nearby park and enjoy the same wandering process. Don't ask a park ranger—half the fun is finding a brook yourselves. If it's warm enough, take a dip, or at least splash your toes in the sparkling waters.

Go to a Petting Zoo

It is one thing to visit a regular zoo, but it is a very different experience to actually touch, hold, pet, and cuddle baby animals. Going to a petting zoo will bring out your desire to be more nurturing and

tactile with each other. Doing something like holding a baby monkey or feeding a baby goat his bottle will immediately soften even the hardest cynic. When we are out in the world trying to be smart, sophisticated human beings, we often lose sight of our very basic nature. Being around baby animals helps us get in touch with our instinctual loving feelings. When you and your lover share this experience it will open up the pathways to a greater, more loving, connection.

Witness the Miracle of Birth

There is nothing more romantic than witnessing the miracle of birth. If you don't know any women who are expecting this spring, you and your lover have other options. With its long, flowing mane and graceful, rhythmic gait, the horse is one of nature's most beautiful, romantic creatures. In the springtime, foals are born to brood mares everywhere (for those of you lacking in equine knowledge, a pony is a separate breed, it is NOT a baby horse!) You and your lover can go to any farm or stable in your area to watch this profound process taking place. If you can't find a farm or stable near you, then call a racetrack or local veterinarian. One of those sources should definitely be able to point you in the right direction. You and your lover might even want to be there for the naming of the foal or come back a week later to see how the baby is doing. By staying in touch with the farmer or the trainer, you can even track the progress of the foal through it's life and see where it ends up. Who knows, your little baby might just turn out to be a big winner! If horses don't appeal to you, or you are allergic, then see if you can find someone with a pregnant cat or dog. Offer to help find good homes for the newborn pups or kittens. This gives the two of you a loving task to work on together. The two of you can each put posters up in your office, at a local school, gym, bus stop, or church. Doing something like this helps take the focus off of the "everyday grind" of your relationship, and helps spread the joy around.

Build a Tree House

This is another activity from childhood that can become incredibly romantic when you try it again as an adult. Both of you should share equally in picking out a spot, buying the materials, and building the house. You may want to paint the house pink or stripe it with a rainbow of colors. The tree house is supposed to be a secret romantic hideaway, where you can go to escape the world. It is for the two of you to enjoy with a childlike freedom. Once the house is built, try to go there as much as possible. The tree house can be a great place for quiet reflection, meditation, or fooling around. Whatever activities you and your lover choose to do, your tree house should always be a place of peace, love, passion, and tranquillity.

Pedal Pushers: Go for a Bike Ride

This is a physically healthy and romantic thing to do on a fresh spring day. There's nothing like getting your blood pumping as you and your loved one ride bikes in a park, by a lake, or even just through the streets of your town. Bike riding offers a chance to discover new places and things that you can easily miss when driving around in a car. To really be romantic, why not take a whirl on a bicycle built for two? That way you'll really get to enjoy your teamwork!

The Love Boat

Set sail on a romantic voyage built for two! Enjoy a lazy spring afternoon canoeing gently downstream, or take a rowboat out on a tranquil lake and each take one oar so you can sit side by side. For the more daring, pack a lunch and some drinks and rent a sailboat for the day. Go out into the ocean or just loll around the harbor. For those of

you who live in Florida, California, or the Caribbean, try a Hoby Catamaran, which is for warm waters only. If neither of you know how to sail, then take a sailing lesson at least one or two times before you venture out on your own.

Sunrise, Sunset

In the springtime, the sun begins to shine much earlier than in the winter months, so why not be there to usher in the dawn of the new day? Find out from your local newspaper or television news at what time the sun will rise. Set your alarm clock and go to a beautiful outdoor spot, or enjoy watching the sunrise from the comfort of a spot on your own property, or even from a window that faces east. On a weekend, make a date to have cocktails together at sunset. This is nature's way of helping the two of you stop what you are doing and engage in romance at least twice a day!

Frolic in the Fields

To let off some steam and stress from the week, find a big, open field and run through it! You can skip together hand in hand, stop to pick flowers, or yell and howl with wild abandon. If there is a field near you where baby lambs are grazing, you will find that they make great playmates. Run through a field with lambs and watch them run with you. You and your lover may even want to stop and pick clover. You know what they say, make a wish on a four leaf clover and watch all your romantic dreams come true!

A Spring Bouquet

Picking or cutting a spring flower bouquet may seem like a very simple thing to do, but actually it is an age-old practice. Enjoy picking beautiful flowers from your own garden or go to a local nursery for potted blooms. Make lovely, colorful bouquets for your dining room, bedroom, and bathrooms. The arrival of fresh spring flowers in the house always creates a soft, romantic environment. It's like having a constant reminder of new love everywhere you turn.

Visit a Botanical Garden

For the real die-hard spring flower fans, check out the botanical gardens in your area. Sometimes old estates that have been turned into "open-to-the-public" museums also have beautiful manicured gardens for the two of you to ramble through. You can count on a quiet and beguiling atmosphere, surrounded by lush blooms and heady fragrances.

Up, Up, and Away

For the romantic thrill of a lifetime, sail over land and sea in a hot air balloon. You'll see the world as you never have before. Spend the day, or just go for an hour or two. Gliding through the air, you and your lover will experience a sense of uninhibited freedom. The two of you can take turns screaming "I Love You" at the top of your lungs for all of the world to hear!

Go Camping

There are many different ways to enjoy a romantic camping adventure. For really down-to-earth souls, just grab your sleeping bags and backpacks and head off into the woods. Take your time cooking dinner and roasting marshmallows over an open fire, while you share funny stories about your childhood camping adventures and mishaps. Needless to say, end the evening by making love under the stars. For those of you city sophisticates who only like a little bit of the outdoors, rent a camper and go to a protected campground. Many campgrounds offer such facilities as electrical outlets, pools, tennis courts, and other sports activities. In these type of campground resorts, you can enjoy the great outdoors without ever having to really rough it.

Go Fish

For lovers who might want to catch their own dinner, fishing can provide a great romantic interlude on a lovely spring day. There are so many things you can do to enjoy this type of outdoorsy afternoon. Below are some creative ways to get a real splash out of fishing!

1. River Fishing

This is a popular sport with English royals as wells as American Yankees. You will need some fishing gear and big, floppy boots. Hand in hand, walk right into the water and cast your baited line. When you feel something bite, reel in the fish together. Have a romantic time conquering your catch.

2. Deep Sea Fishing

If the two of you are die-hard fishermen with a real love of the sea, you will really enjoy this dawn-till-dusk sport. Just rent a boat with a captain and have him take you to a spot in the ocean where the fish are biting. Pack a lunch and some wine, and make a romantic day of it. Later that evening, enjoy sautéing your "catch of the day" and sharing stories of your adventure at sea.

3. Cup Fishing

This is for lovers who like the idea of fishing, but would rather have their sole served to them on a plate. Get some paper cups and head down to your local stream or brook. Take off your shoes, roll up your pants, and stick your feet into the cold water. Enjoy splashing around and skipping stones. Once you get used to the water, find a school of fish and scoop some up in your cups. You can choose to take them home or to set them free. This is a sweet way to have fun fishing without making a big production out of it.

Take a Drive Through the Country

It's always nice to take a little romantic escape. When you don't have time for a long weekend away, a simple drive through the countryside will give you the break that you need. Just hop in your car and drive along some quiet country lanes, stopping to enjoy a picnic and go for a walk. Taking a nice, long drive through the country will help clear your minds and your hearts.

Spring Baskets

If you and your lover are the creative types, you can help spread your springtime love around. Go to a gardening store and buy enough wicker baskets for everyone on your street. Fill the baskets with fresh cut flowers, home-baked goods, and/or brightly colored candy. Attach a card that reads "Have a happy springtime...with love (insert your names)". Leave the baskets on all of your neighbor's doorsteps. They will appreciate the random act of kindness and may even reciprocate by inviting you over for dinner or sending you something special on the next holiday.

Lighten Up

After dressing in the dark grays, blues, and blacks of winter, spring is the perfect time to brighten up your wardrobe. Have a good rummage through your closet and throw out anything that seems old and drab. Go out and buy each other at least one article of outrageously colored clothing, like a really crazy Hawaiian shirt or a multi-colored tie-dyed T-shirt. Try on some funky jewelry to go with your new outfits and buy some cool sneakers. Lighten up your love life by going to an outdoor café in your new spring clothes.

The Circus Is Coming to Town

Take a trip to the circus for an afternoon of mini-escapism. Romance has a great chance to bloom under the big top. Buy yourselves some peanuts or share a cotton candy. What could be more fun for lovers than the greatest show on earth?!

Hi Ho Silver

Horseback riding is a romantic way to experience a true sense of freedom. If you've never ridden a horse before, you may want to take a lesson or two before galloping off into the wild blue yonder. Most horseback riding stables offer a choice between Western and English style saddles, as well as guided trail rides, beach or park rides, or woodsy sleepovers. For serious equine enthusiasts, take a horseback riding vacation—a seven-day trek through the green fields of Ireland or up into the romantic hills of Tuscany, or, closer to home, try a dude ranch in Wyoming or Arizona.

Horsing Around

If you like the idea of being around horses, but don't have the nerve to mount one yourself, there are many romantic ways to spend a spring afternoon with your lover "just horsing around." Here are some suggestions:

1. Polo

Often called the sport of kings, you can find a good polo game in Santa Barbara, Bridgehampton, Palm Beach, Connecticut, Long Island, or at a stable near you. This event often draws celebrities, such as Sylvester Stallone and Stephanie Seymour. In England, all three Princes—Charles, William, and Harry—can be seen enjoying polo almost every weekend. Park your car, open up the trunk, and enjoy some champagne, a "Pims Cup," and a "hamper lunch" consisting of smoked Scotch salmon, deviled eggs, carved turkey and ham, caviar, and croissants. Depending on the match you attend, you may be required to dress up in what is known in upper-crust circles as "polo lunch attire." This means silk dresses and big hats for the ladies and ties and navy blue blazers for the gentlemen. It is also quite possible that attending a polo game is a quiet casual affair where shorts and T-shirts will suffice. At half-time, you and your lover can enjoy "stomping divots" or walking around the field.

2. And They're Off

Horse racing is another fun, romantic, and exciting spectator sport. Act like a champion owner and take a walk around the paddock to inspect the horses before they gallop their way down the racetrack. Have a fancy lunch in the clubroom or just share some track-side sandwiches as you cheer on your favorite horse and jockey. Take turns making bets and giving each other the money if you have a lucky day. After spending the day at the races, you and your lover will both come home feeling like big winners.

3. Be a Real Show-off

Horse shows are another fast-paced, exciting equine event that can have you and your lover jumping in your seats. Catch a thrill watching those 4,000-pound graceful creatures hurling themselves over six-foot fences, water jumps, and tricky "ins and outs." Show jumping is like a speed-timed obstacle course. You'll be left breathless as you watch horse and rider try to beat the clock. The competition is fierce and the stakes are high. You and your lover can't help but feel part of the action.

Duck, Duck, Goose

Sometimes the simplest pleasures can be the most romantic of all. Find a duck pond in your area and spend a quiet afternoon feeding the ducks, relaxing in the sunshine, and basking in the springtime glow of each

other's company. This is an easy way to share intimacy without the interruptions and intrusions of the busy world. You will actually have the time to talk about things you haven't discussed in a while and learn new things about each other that you didn't know before. Use this time to reconnect, recharge, and reclaim your love for each other.

Fore!

Golf is a great game for a bright spring day. Because it is a rather "slow" sport, you can really savor the time you spend together. Have fun driving around in the golf cart or take advantage of the nice weather and walk around the course. Alternatively, find yourselves a wacky miniature golf course. Golf is a good couple's sport because it doesn't have to bring out your competitive natures to be thoroughly enjoyed. You two can really work as a team as you learn to play. Afterwards, enjoy a lavish lunch at a golf club or an ice cream cone on a bench at the miniature golf course.

Kick It

For those of you who like some "rough and tumble" to get you going on a spring day, have yourselves a ball playing a little one-on-one soccer. Go to your local park and use some fallen branches to act as goal posts. Once you've marked your territory, really go for it as you vigorously try to take the ball away from each other. Playing a game of active sports is not only a great way to work up a sweat, but it is also a safe and healthy way to let out any pent-up aggression you may be harboring. The best way to keep a love relationship happy and romantic is to get rid of any negative energy before it gets the best of you. You and your lover will also benefit from the adrenaline you get when you play a high action contact sport. This can immediately put you in the mood for love.

And the Winner Is...

The Oscars is perhaps Hollywood's most romantic event. The Academy Award Show is a no-holds-barred evening of glitz and glamour where love is always in the spotlight. Even if you and your lover live a million miles away from the celebrity star-fest, you can still enjoy a romantic awards ceremony of your own. The Oscars is aired around the same time in March every year. Your local novelty shop will usually carry fake Oscar statues that say things like "Best Mom," "Best Friend," or "Best Lover" on them. On Oscar night, you and your lover can take turns being the presenter and the recipient of this illustrious award as you have the real ceremony playing on the television in the background. You can even make up the categories that you are awarding each other for. You may want to give your lover the "Best Smoocher" or "Best Massage" award. Be really creative and personal with your "Oscars," because what you are really doing is taking advantage of this ceremony to acknowledge your lover's special qualities. Each of you should also have an acceptance speech prepared. Thank your lover for treating you and making you feel like a celebrity everyday. Toast the end of the night with champagne and caviar as you go off to your bedroom to enjoy your private "after-party."

Taking It to the Streets

An offbeat romantic thing to do on a lovely May day is to wander aimlessly through a street fair. Have fun exploring all the funky little booths, looking at the arts and crafts, eating street vendor food, and listening to curb-side musicians. A street fair can make your own boring neighborhood come alive with romance. If you're ambitious, you and your lover might even enjoy participating in the street fair with a booth of your own. Perhaps you bake killer chocolate chip cookies that you always wanted to try selling, but never had a venue. Maybe your lover is great with ceramics or secretly always wanted to

be a painter. A street fair is great romantic way for you and your lover to express individual creativity while sharing the experience.

Garage Sale

No, this is not just for grandmothers anymore. Scrounging through garage sales is a great way to find unique little romantic knick-knacks that you would never be able to find in a department store. If it is the first time that you two are decorating a home together, or even if you are just giving the old place a much needed "spring spruce-up," you can find items in a garage sale that have romantic personal flair. The next time you and your lover see a tag sale, take a minute and start picking!

New Artist

Whenever you and your lover try something new together it is a special event! To have a truly romantic cultural experience, go to an art exhibition that is featuring ONLY the works of new artists. Have a great time looking at the paintings or sculptures and trying to figure out who is going to be the next Picasso or Miro. If you can afford it, buy a piece of new art together and keep it as an investment. That way if the artist becomes famous, you can say you "knew him when."

Veg Out

Since spring is a time for all things green to grow, many restaurants offer a "spring vegetable" tasting menu. This gives the chef a chance to be innovative with the very freshest of veggies and produce this time of year has to offer. You and your lover will enjoy going for a healthy, gourmet spring dinner and sampling the chef's latest creations. Maybe you would have more fun if you were your own chefs and made a springtime veggie meal together. Just go to the vegetable and produce section of your local supermarket and ask someone who works there what is currently in season. Look in a cookbook to get ideas or experiment on your own.

Life Is a Cabaret

As the song goes, "What good is sitting alone in your room, come hear the music play." For a change of pace in your normal entertainment, find yourselves a smoky cabaret featuring music from the '40s and '50s. As you have a couple of drinks and listen to the singer belt out the blues, the seedy environment will seduce you.

Totally Wig Out

You don't have to wait for Halloween to have fun with costumes. You and your lover can have a blast just going to your local wig store and trying them on. Ever wondered what your lover would look like with red curly hair or a brown straight bob? Have you always wished you had the nerve to have big hair like Dolly Parton? Indulge in fantasy by making yourselves look like other people. If you want to take your dress-up game a step further, then take a bunch of wigs home and play with them in privacy. This is sure to add a bit of unknown danger and excitement to your romance!

I'm Dreaming of You

Our dreams tell us many things about our lives, ourselves, and our romantic relationships. Some dreams have been known to have real predictive qualities. Did you ever wonder what your dreams were trying to tell you? If you and your lover want to remember your dreams, New York City expert dream analyst Sam Daniels suggests that you do the following things:

❧ **DRINK A BIG GLASS OF WATER BEFORE YOU GO TO BED.**

❧ **IMAGINE A CLEAR, BLUE LIGHT CIRCLING YOUR THROAT AS YOU FALL ASLEEP (THIS IS GIVING POSITIVE ENERGY TO YOUR COMMUNICATION.**

KEEP A PEN AND SOME PAPER BY YOUR BED, SO YOU CAN WRITE DOWN WHAT YOU REMEMBER AS SOON AS YOU WAKE UP.

After you and your lover have entered a couple of weeks' worth of notes in your "dream journals," you may decide to have them professionally analyzed, or buy a book on dream analysis and do it yourselves. The purpose of doing this is to gain a deeper insight into the desires of each other's subconscious minds. This will bring you much closer and strengthen your romantic ties.

Let the Spirit Move You

If you and your lover practice the same religion or share similar spiritual beliefs, then you may want to spend the weekend attending a spiritual retreat. Many of the Christian faiths offer religious-centered getaways at retreat centers nationwide. If you are a member of the Jewish faith, ask your rabbi or community center about attending a spiritual "Shabbatone." Either a temple or Jewish families who study Kabbalah, the mystical side of Judaism, will host a "Shabbatone." If you are more interested in spiritualism (or metaphysics) than organized religion, go to your local bookstore or health food store to find out about a New Age discovery center in your area. Whatever your personal beliefs, you and your lover will benefit greatly from a weekend of reflection and heartfelt contemplation. You will come away from the weekend knowing the deeper meaning of two souls that are in love.

She Blinded Me with Science

When was the last time you and your lover talked about the magnitude of our solar system or tried to defy the laws of gravity? Like most grown-ups, you probably have not been on a scientific adventure since grade school. You and your lover will get a kick out of spending the afternoon in your local science museum or planetarium. You two will be amazed all over again by the exhibits and learning how the world works. You will also probably enjoy talking about something other than your work and your relationship. Going to a science museum with your lover will remind you that we are all part of a miraculous universe.

Take an Art Class

If admiring the work of new artists has inspired you to get in touch with your creative side, then why not sign up for an art class together? You can learn to paint, draw, or sculpt each other out of clay. When you start to get proficient, take turns modeling nude for one another. Developing your artistic talents will help you and your lover enjoy a wealth of uninhibited expression.

Cause and Effect

Is there a social issue that you really believe in or have a strong feeling about, but never had the time to make an effort? You and your lover can join forces to let the public know just how you feel. Whether it's animal rights or you want the government to close down a nuclear power plant near you, it is time to speak out and let your voice be heard. Joining or starting a peaceful protest will show your lover how passionate you can become about an issue that you really care about. No doubt this will add a new level of romantic excitement to your own relationship. So go ahead and save those whales, while you show your lover that you know the real meaning of "passion."

Hold the Pickle

Eating lunch outside with your lover on a gorgeous spring day is a great way to break up the monotony of your long working hours. Skip the cafeteria or the fancy restaurant and meet each other by the food stand or push cart. Share a sloppy hot dog dripping with mustard or

a salty pretzel in the sunshine. The focus of your lunchtime interlude should be the intimacy that you enjoy together. Revel in the romantic simplicity of your "push-cart date." Sneak a few kisses as you wipe the relish off your lover's cheek before you have to go back to the office.

Hark!

To take a romantic escape into another place and time, check out a springtime medieval or Renaissance festival. You and your lover can pretend that you are "lord and lady" as you explore the music, theme dances, poetry, art, and food from Old England. While you are at the festival, challenge each other to speak in an English accent. The first one who slips up or forgets has to read a Shakespeare sonnet five times in a row.

Springtime Resolutions

While it is true that people generally make their resolutions on New Year's, spring is actually the perfect time of year to "start over." Since spring is a time of rebirth and renewal, why not make changes to improve your life and your love? If you are married, then take this time to renew your vows. If you are dating, then make a list of romantic things that you two are going to do for or with each other.

Work it Out

If you and your lover made a resolution to get in shape all the way back in January, spring is the perfect time to renew this commitment to good health. Since the bikini season of summer is soon coming around to bite you two on your butts, why not hit the gym together and work your bodies? If you absolutely hate to go to the gym, then make a date to go jogging, power walking, or hiking at least three or four times a week. An added bonus to working out is that you will enjoy a natural high that can lead to great sex later on.

He's A Swingin' Guy

Guess what, lovers? Swinging is back! Now wipe those smiles off your faces and get your minds out of the gutter. Swing dancing to the big band sounds of the 1940s has made a big comeback and is becoming a new and improved favorite among a new generation of "swingers." Check your local churches, concert halls, or community centers and ask about "swing dance night." If they don't already have one planned, you and your lover might volunteer to start one. Don't worry about being klutzy, it doesn't even matter if you've never been a good dancer before. Swing dancing is fun and easy. By swinging around the room and enjoying the wonderful music, you and your lover will be transported to a simpler, more innocent, romantic time in our national history.

The Grand Ol' Opry

Country music has more romantic tunes and lyrics than perhaps any other style of music in the world. Go to the record store and pick out some favorite country albums. Listen to them for a while to really get the pacing of the singers' voices plus the feel of the rhythm. With the music of your choice quietly playing in the background, sit down and write your lover a country tune, then sing your heart out (oh yes, you have to sing it, too!)

Romance, She Wrote

If you are the literary sort, why not sit down and write a novel starring you and your lover? Believe it or not, becoming your own personal author is a lot easier than you would imagine, even if you failed English class. To tell your own Lover's Story, just sit down and write the story of how you first met and what first attracted you to each other. Tell some of the funny stories that you share together, and some of the romantic things you have enjoyed as well. It doesn't have

to be perfect, because this story is only for the two of you to read. It will bring you closer as you have a chance to relive your most romantic times. Also, if you and your lover ever have a huge fight, a little lover's quarrel, or are thinking of breaking up (heaven forbid), then you can re-read this book and think about all the wonderful times you've shared together, before you do anything drastic. This book will also be a lovely memento to share with your children one day if romantic fate takes you and your lover down that road. For those of you with a real creative streak, you can write a series of novellas placing you and your lover in dangerously romantic situations around the world. To achieve even more romantic glory, sit down and write your love story together.

Hi-Ya!

This spring, you and your lover might enjoy doing something to build your mental and physical strength—a beginner's martial arts class. Since you can't be together to protect each other 100 percent of the time, then why not do something that will make you both stronger and healthier people? No matter where you live in the United States, you should be able to easily find martial arts classes (beginner classes included) by looking in the Yellow Pages or checking online. Martial arts is probably the least violent and most honorable form of self-protection. When you and your lover realize how strong and powerful you both are, it will add a whole other dimension of attraction to the relationship.

Zoom Zoom

Need something this spring besides your lover to make your heart start to race? For the thrill-seeking romantic couples who have to live and love on the edge, how about learning to drive a racecar this spring? You don't have to go to the Monaco Grand Prix or the Indie 500 to get behind the wheel of a hot rod. Just call your local auto association to find the race track nearest you. You and your lover will fly like the wind around the track as you learn to master this very dangerous sport. Lovers-turned-racers can become addicted to this sport very quickly. So grab your honey, strap on your helmet, and get ready for a springtime experience!

March in a Parade

Since the weather is so inviting during the springtime, this is the perfect time for a parade, complete with marching bands and cheering crowds. Watch from the sidelines or follow along and get in on the action. No matter what the cause for the parade is, you and your lover can get into the spring spirit and enjoy them all. This spring, break out your old set of high school pompoms or make new ones. If you or your lover play a portable instrument like a flute, drums, or horn, this is a great opportunity to get in touch with your musical side. A springtime parade, whether you watch or march, is an energetic way for you and your lover to regain that special sense of enthusiasm.

Let's Go to the Hop

Enjoy a retro-trip back to the 1950s—throw an old fashioned "Sock Hop" for your friends and family, or just for the two of you. Pick up a CD that has the biggest hits of the '50s; that way you'll have a variety of tunes. You may also want to pick up some romantic Elvis records or videos of some of his movies (check out *Blue Hawaii*) playing in the background. Make some red Jello punch (spike it if you want to) and serve up peanut butter and jelly, or baloney on white bread. Don't forget the Cheese Whiz on Ritz Crackers! Dress in '50s clothing and have a ball!

THE SPRINGTIME VACATION

Spring is the perfect time to plan a romantic getaway. Whether it's a long weekend in the country or a two-week sailing soiree, a springtime escape can be exactly what you need to shake the cobwebs out of your relationship. So grab your lover, take a deep breath, and head for the hills, fields, streams, or lakes, or have yourselves a bright-lights, big-city romance.

Crisp Weather Romantic Spring Vacation Spots

1. Oooh La La Paris!

Ah, gay Paris! What could be more romantic in the spring than a sexy weekend in the City of Lights. Stroll hand-in-hand by the Seine and spend cozy nights sipping wine at the George V. Wander around the majestic halls of the Palais Versailles or wipe flakes of freshly baked buttery croissants off each others' chins at a café on the Left Bank. When it comes to romance, the French are famous—why not immerse yourselves in the capitol city of romance?

2. The Big Apple

Spring in New York City is the perfect big-city romance. The weather is cool and inviting, which means the parks, museums, and outdoor cafés are brimming with energetic New Yorkers. Treat your lover to a picnic in Central Park, a boat trip at The Boat House and, of course, a hansom cab ride to the Plaza Hotel for tea and goodies in the romantic Palm Court room. When night falls, take your Broadway baby to a show on the Great White Way (don't forget to tell your lover that he will always be the star of your show). Have a celebrity-sighting after-theater dinner at Sardi's, or split a huge steak at Frankie and Johnny's. New York is a "big town" that sets the stage for a "big-time" spring romance.

3. Cliveden, Taplow, England

Cliveden was once the English home of a rich American high society family. This is where one of the greatest international, aristocratic "forbidden" romances took place almost century ago (long before Prince Charles and Camilla Parker-Bowles). Today the luscious grounds and spectacular castle on the Cliveden grounds have been transformed into a luxurious hotel and spa. Each guestroom has an unbelievable view of the rolling English countryside, and is large enough for your own private party. Perhaps the most romantic thing about Cliveden is that there is absolutely nothing to do there but relax and be treated like a king or queen. Get lost walking around the great grounds like real country dwellers, or ask the butler to arrange for a horseback tour. Dine on gourmet fare in the blue and gold French-inspired dining room, or feed each other dainty finger sandwiches in your big en-suite marble bath tubs. If all the romping around the large feather beds have exhausted you and your lover, then have a swim in the pool or try one of the many European Spa treatments offered. You and your lover will feel as if you have been transported into another place and time. At Cliveden, indeed you have!

4. The Netherlands

With the picturesque windmills and the tulips in full bloom, Amsterdam and the surrounding areas are irresistible during the spring. Take in the gorgeous flowers as you glide down the Amstel River in your own private paddleboat. In the evening, you and your lover can discover the "naughty" side of the city. Amsterdam has earned an international reputation for being the capital of "free love" and uninhibited sexuality. If the two of you are daring enough, give each other permission to do things you wouldn't ordinarily do if you were anywhere else but in Amsterdam.

5. Washington, D.C.

The blooming cherry blossoms are part of what makes our nation's capital so lovely and romantic during the springtime. The Lincoln Memorial and all our other national treasures are so much more beautiful this time of year. Sometimes just being in the powerful aura of where it all happens can be an intense aphrodisiac. You and your lover will want to explore the White House and other government buildings, or retire early back to your hotel to cause a big romantic scandal of your own. Listen carefully to birds chirping outside your window—rumor has it that they know all the latest gossip on Capitol Hill. In the evening, you and your lover can stroll down the cobblestone streets of Georgetown or sneak off to an after-hours night club with a real international flair. With a lot of passion and a little diplomacy, in Washington, D.C., you and your lover can have an absolutely Presidential affair.

6. Williamsburg, Virginia

The state of Virginia's slogan is "Virginia is for lovers." That statement couldn't be more true, especially around springtime. Williamsburg is a lovely little town that has been completely restored to the 1770s. For you history buffs, or for those of you patriots who feel that you missed out on the Revolution, Williamsburg is the hottest thing since the Boston Tea Party. You and your lover can actually experience what it was like to live in George Washington's time. Romantic times, indeed.

7. To Romania, With Love

Now that the Iron Curtain is gone, Eastern Europe's beautiful old cities have been thoroughly modernized to meet the comfort needs of the Western traveler. Romania—home to the serene Transylvanian Mountains, stately old "dashas" (homes), and the romantic seaside town of Timashora—offers lovers a romantic getaway off the beaten track. What most people don't know is that

Romania has always been a pioneer in the development of spa treatments. Long before America was filled with fancy spas, Romanian doctors and practitioners were helping lovers of all ages recapture their strength and youth. Romania also offers delicious Baltic cuisine that includes fresh sturgeon, handmade salami, and piles and piles of black and red caviar. For a change of pace and a one-of-a-kind spring getaway, grab your baby and fly to Bucharest. You and your lover will have a red hot Romanian romance!

8. I Left My Heart…in San Francisco

The "frisky city" on the edge of the Pacific is full of romantic things to do. You and your lover can take a boat out into the Bay, then head to the wooden piers of Fisherman's Wharf for a carousel ride, a glass of red wine, and the catch of the day. San Francisco is a town that's built for lovers and "foodies," so don't forget to stuff yourselves silly at a homemade fudge stand or at the Ghirardelli Chocolate outpost in Cannery Wharf. End the day with a breathless up-and-down ride over the city's steep hills in a famous trolley. Before you head to the airport, see if you can grab a Sunday brunch on top of the Fairmont hotel. Not only will you and your lover taste some of the freshest poached salmon you've ever had, you will also enjoy spectacular views of the city.

9. Nashville

This spring, why don't you and that special someone set your hearts to music? Take the one you love to a night at the Grand Old Opry to hear one of America's country superstars serenade the audience with a sad, soppy song. After the concert, dive into a romantic down-home meal of fried chicken, black eye peas, grits, and sweet corn bread. Take a few hours' drive out to Graceland to see the former home of the king of rock 'n roll. Yes ma'am! While away an afternoon just sitting in a rocker on the front porch of a Belle Meade antebellum mansion with a mint julep in your hand.

You and your lover will be sweetly soothed by the sublime graciousness of this deep southern town.

10. New Orleans

Nowhere on this earth is there a more sultry, seductive oasis than the city of New Orleans. Mardi Gras aside, New Orleans is a wild town existing purely for the pursuit of pleasure. Maybe it's the thickness of the humid air, the hot bluesy jazz clubs, or the bourbon-soaked festivities that run deep into the night. No one really knows exactly why New Orleans brings out the party animal in lovers. It's one of the great mysteries of the south. Everything in New Orleans is specifically geared to satisfy the lustiest cravings.

Warm Weather Spring Vacation Hot Spots

1. Bermuda Shorts

Just a little bit over an hour's flight from the East Coast, or a five-day cruise from New York, Bermuda offers a nearby island getaway. Since Bermuda is on the same latitude as North Carolina, it is not quite as warm and steamy as the islands of the Caribbean. Also, since Bermuda was an English Colony, it still possesses an interesting mix of "proper British" formality and tropical island relaxation. The sands at Elbow Beach are pearly white, and the water is a tempting shade of aquamarine blue. Learning to swim with the dolphins can be an unbelievably romantic experience. Bermuda is perfect for lovers who like good service and don't like to feel stranded, but crave a little bit of paradise.

2. Puerto Rico, You Lovely Island!

Want a little Latin romance to put some "salsa" back into your step? The good news is that you don't have to schlep all the way to Spain to enjoy a hot tango for two. Puerto Rico has a sizzling, sexy

Latin identity all it's own. Spend your days sunning on the pristine beaches or getting to know Old San Juan. Hot nights can be spent learning to Flamenco dance or trying your luck in one of the many casinos. You and your lover will come back from San Juan with satisfied smiles on both your faces. Olé!

3. Casa de Campo

Once an exclusive Costa Rican enclave for the royal, rich, and famous, Casa de Campo in La Romana has opened its island doors to anyone who wants to live like a king. Casa de Campo is an aristocratic magnet for the elite. Still privately owned by the Fanjuls, Florida's wealthiest sugar family, Casa de Campo is a sweet Caribbean escape from mundane reality. Wander aimlessly along the beaches or do something unusual like learn to play polo. Hide under a palm tree behind dark sunglasses pretending to escape the paparazzi, or play nine holes on their amazing golf course. Casa de Campo will give you and your lover much more than a glimpse of the good life.

4. Playa del Carmen, Mexico

This exotic location just thirty or so miles south of Cancun is currently becoming "the place to be" on the Mexican Riviera. Sneak away for a romantic siesta at the new Deseo Hotel, a chic getaway with only fifteen rooms, where the official color is white. You will feel as though you are staying in your own private villa. Playa del Carmen is not a place for lovers who want peace and quiet. This is a nonstop party haven with endless cocktails, beach parties, and loud music that plays into the wee hours of the morning. You and your lover can be a part of the new emerging international scene as you indulge in a tequila-soaked romance.

5. South Beach, Miami Beach, Florida

Some say it's over and others say it has endless lives. Whatever your viewpoint, no one can deny that Miami's South Beach is the

hottest "see and be seen" spot in America. Miami's perfect spring-time beach weather, gorgeous sunsets, and blue waters make South Beach the perfect place for a romantic "happening" couple. Spend days soaking up the sun or roller-blading down the infamous Ocean Drive. Romantic nights can consist of grabbing dinner at any of the celebrity-splattered restaurants and dancing the night away at the nonstop night clubs. If you're lucky, you can catch a ride on a private yacht and take a tour around the bay. For the romantic couple who loves a "tourist-driven" vacation, check out local zoos, parks, the Bayside Mall, the Everglades, and many other nearby attractions.

6. Langkawi, Penane, Maldives

Far away on a secluded beach facing the Andamam Sea, The Detai Hotel in Kendah Darul Aman (in the northwest of Langkawi) offers a romantic retreat for lovers who want an escape to "the ends of the earth." You and your lover will be secluded in an ancient tropical rainforest surrounded by exotic foliage and wildlife. Hire a guide and discover something new in a very old place, lose yourselves in the natural surroundings, or take advantage of the healing rainforest remedies offered at the Mandara spa. When you and your lover return from the lush hideaway, you will feel refreshed and ready to take on the hectic pace of your everyday lives.

7. Seoul, South Korea

The Shilla hotel in Seoul, South Korea is a romantic garden paradise located smack in the middle of the city. You and your lover can meander around the extensive sculpture gardens that surround the incredible property. If you are in the mood to experiment with some traditional Korean cuisine, savor the creations of the Shilla's gourmet chef. Afterwards, spend time touring the ancient and modern areas of Seoul's downtown. Many celebrities and heads of state from around the world have lovingly named the Shilla "the

Korean Buckingham Palace." If you and your lover favor the out-of-the-ordinary romantic springtime vacation, a trip to Korea will lighten your heart.

8. Israel

Lovers of all religions will enjoy a historic romantic getaway in the heart of Israel. Whether you choose to pray at the Wailing Wall, walk the path of Christ in Jerusalem, or enjoy a café and shopping in the Deisengof section of Tel Aviv, Israel offers the perfect mixture of ancient history and modern cosmopolitan life. Pamper yourselves with a weekend at the luxurious King David Hotel or bravely climb Masada and visit the Kumran Caves at sun-up. Enjoy a therapeutic mud fight and astounding views of Jordan when you take a trip to the Dead Sea. Israel is also home to miles of sun-drenched beaches, especially in the cities of Natanya, Elat, and Tel Aviv. For some lovers, going to Israel results in finding a spiritual home. No matter how you two choose to spend your time in this special place, a trip to Israel will restore your faith in love and romance. *L'chaim!*

9. Viva Las Vegas

If you and your sweetie are higher-rollers in love, take a springtime trip to the tackiest romantic city in the world. Spring is one of the best seasons in Vegas, because it is much warmer than the winter and has not yet reached its scorching desert summer temperatures. Whether you choose to gamble the night away at one of the many hotel casinos, stuff yourselves at an all-you-can-eat buffet, or catch an eye-popping show, Las Vegas offers action and excitement twenty-four hours a day, three hundred-and-sixty-five days a year. When you need a break from the nonstop commotion, take a romantic helicopter tour over the Grand Canyon, then relax in an oversized heart-shaped bathtub back in your hotel's honeymoon suite. Who knows, your time in Vegas could be so romantic

that you may find yourselves standing before a velvet-clad J.P. in the Elvis Chapel. If you and your lover make a last minute decision to tie the knot, Las Vegas is prepared and ready to help you do it at a moment's notice. Just speak to your hotel's concierge and believe it or not, you can have a cake, flowers, dress, private reception, and marriage license organized for you all within twenty-four hours.

March

St. Patrick's Day (March 17th)

This is a carefree, "party" day when, regardless your ethnic heritage, everybody is Irish. On St. Paddy's day, everyone has a license to have a great time! There are several ways to catch the St. Patrick's Day spirit and revel in the green-themed atmosphere of fun.

ROLL OVER YOUR FOUR-LEAF CLOVER

Go searching in a park or field for a four-leaf clover. You and your lover will have so much fun searching for one, that it won't matter if can't find what you are looking for. Don't be afraid to cheat a little bit and make your own. Just pick two clovers and put them together or split one of the clover leaves in half. Take turns making three romantic wishes on the clover. You can either bury the clover in a special place after you make your wishes or, if you want to go all out, you can make a "clover keepsake" by laminating your make-shift four-leaf clover onto a wallet-sized piece of paper, on the back of which you've written both your names and your romantic wishes. Keep your special clovers in your wallets until next St. Patrick's Day. Have fun looking back and seeing which romantic wishes came true.

THE JIG IS UP

Riverdance and *Lord of The Dance* are filled with mind-blowing music and athletic Irish dancing. You and your lover can check out one of these shows or rent the video. Try dancing along, or see if you can find a dancing school that will teach you both how to dance an Irish jig.

THE ST. PADDY'S DAY FEAST

End this merry day with a lavish Irish feast. Pour yourselves two pints of Guinness Stout, the official drink of Ireland (easy to find at your local liquor store or supermarket). Then spend the evening listening to romantic Irish music from Enya, or U2 if you prefer more intense music, while you bake Irish soda bread and whip up a lamb stew or corned beef and cabbage. To get the recipes for these traditional goodies, check out any Irish cookbook or website. Call your local bakery and ask if they are selling green cupcakes in honor of the holiday. This is a warm, romantic way to end this lively day.

First Day Of Spring (March 21st)

The vernal equinox marks the first day of spring. By doing something special on this day, you and your lover can romantically acknowledge the beginning of this inspiring season. Spend time together celebrating spring—cook a special breakfast and take an early morning walk. Even if it's still a little cold out, see if you can smell spring in the air, that moist earth smell that will make the two of you want to frisk and romp!

Spring Vacation

Remember those wonderful spring break days in college when you'd go somewhere and party with all your friends? Well, even if those days are long gone, you and your sweetie should take at least one springtime day of rest and relaxation. Use a weekend day, or take a personal day at work. Spend the day hand-in-hand, puttering around the garden, or lazing together in bed. Really use this day to relax and regenerate mind, body, and soul. Use the day for a "relationship time out." That does not mean to spend the day apart. Spend the day together, but give each other a break from any negative issues, arguments, or discussions that you may be working through. Instead, talk about all the good things in your relationship, and what makes it all worthwhile. Be thankful for having someone so wonderful in your life.

ROMANTIC SIGN

PISCES (February 19th – March 20th)
Symbol: Two Fish Swimming In Opposite Directions
Rules: The feet
Ruling Planet: Jupiter
Gem Stone: Black Opal
Good Characteristics: polite, mystical, spiritual, generous, social, inspiring, romantic, charismatic in a non-threatening way, into personal enlightenment.
Bad Characteristics: restless, can be easily fooled, can be bad with money, doesn't take career that seriously, can get left behind, doesn't take action.
Romantic Catch Phrase: "You are heaven sent."
What It Means: "I feel the presence of God when I am around you."
What It Really Means: "Being with you is a religious experience."

Top Ten Gifts for a Pisces:
1. Music by Enya.
2. Any book by The Dalai Lama.
3. *Soul Love* by Sanaya Roman.
4. A weekend at a yoga retreat or ashram.
5. Yoga lessons.
6. Any book on meditation.
7. A trip to the Vatican or to Jerusalem.
8. A psychic or aura reading.
9. Tickets to "Crossing Over," the John Edwards Show.

10. A weekend at Deepak Chopra's Ayurvedic spa in La Jolla, California, or any book by Deepak Chopra.

AFRICAN ASTROLOGY SYMBOL:

The Family (March 6th– April 4th)
Body Type: Women are voluptuous with large breasts, men tend to be round in the middle.

Personality Traits: Family oriented, warm, loving, caring, nurturing, non-judgmental, caregivers, know how to share.

Most Romantic Gift: A family photo album.

Favorite Colors: Deep rich blues and burgundies.

How To Win His Heart Forever: Tell him that you are ready to start a family with him.

April

April Fool's Day (April 1st)

The first day of April can be a great time for lovers to have some laughs! (Please be careful when you are teasing each other not to cross the line too much! For example, don't call your lover at work and say, "It's over," and definitely don't call your husband at work and say "I'm having an affair.") There are many ways to poke fun at each other without causing a catastrophe. Here are some ideas:

- REPLACE THE FAVORITE CDS IN HIS OR HER CAR WITH ALL ROMANTIC MUSIC. IF THE CAR HAS A TAPE PLAYER, TAPE A LOVE MESSAGE FROM YOU AND HAVE HIM PLAY IT ON THE WAY TO WORK.

- CALL HER AT WORK AND SAY THAT SHE'S WON THE LOTTERY... THE LOTTERY OF LOVE, THAT IS! YOU MAKE UP THE PRIZE.

- WHEN HE GETS HOME, GREET HIM AT THE DOOR IN AN OLD, WORN-OUT ROBE AND FUZZY SLIPPERS. TELL HIM THAT YOU HAVE A HEADACHE AND ARE NOT IN THE MOOD FOR LOVE. WHEN HE GETS COMFORTABLE IN FRONT OF THE TV, WHIP OFF YOUR ROBE TO REVEAL SEXY LINGERIE, AND ATTACK HIM!

- TELL HIM THAT YOU ARE PUTTING HIM ON A STRICT DIET, THEN SURPRISE HIM WITH A HOME-COOKED GOURMET MEAL. TELL HIM THAT ONLY THE BEST IS GOOD ENOUGH FOR HIM.

- HIDE ALL THE BEER BOTTLES AND BAGS OF CHIPS. REPLACE THEM WITH CHAMPAGNE AND STRAWBERRIES.

Earth Day (April 22nd)

This is a wonderfully romantic day of reconnecting with the Earth. Most areas have some kind of Earth Day celebration ranging from concerts to parades to picnics. If your area doesn't offer some kind of Earth Day festival, you and your lover can start your own. Another romantic thing for you to do is join or start a neighborhood or park clean-up. Think of it as a way of thanking and honoring Mother Earth. End Earth Day by having dinner outdoors and sleeping under the stars.

Easter (varies March-April)

Easter is the most celebrated holiday of spring, marking rebirth and renewal. You may have family obligations on this holiday, but here are also some romantic ways to spend your Easter Sunday.

1. Egg Art
Easter is terrific time for you and your lover to partake in some colorful creative expression. Hard boil some eggs and let them cool. (You can also poke a hole in a raw egg shell and empty out the egg, but empty eggshells are very fragile.) Then take some paint and get to work. Don't be afraid to get inventive with your designs—go crazy using glue, stickers, sparkles, and glitter. Write your names, happy faces, hearts, love notes, or anything else you can fit on the eggs. Enjoy being creative together and having fun like kids.

2. Egg Toss
Start out standing close together, facing each other, and play catch with an egg. The objective is not to drop the egg as you and your lover stand farther and farther apart. Throw the egg lightly, not like a football. Elegance and grace count in an Easter Egg Toss.

3. The Romantic Easter Brunch
You and your lover may want to invite your friends and family over for a lavish Easter brunch. Anytime the two of you entertain

together, it's an opportunity to draw closer and create an expression of your love for each other. Some elegant Easter brunch foods include: smoked salmon, baked Virginia honey glazed ham, a spring vegetable quiche, strawberries in whipped cream, fruit ambrosia, buttery croissants, poppy soufflés, Mimosas, blinis and raspberry tarts. Decorate your Easter table with spring flowers, painted eggs, colored candies, and chocolates. Your guests will be able to tell how much love and thoughtfulness you and your lover put into your Easter brunch and will be anxious to reciprocate!

Passover (varies March-April)

The springtime holiday of Passover celebrates the Hebrew slaves' exodus from Egypt. Also note that in the New Testament, the Last Supper was a Passover Seder. If you and your lover aren't Jewish but have friends who are, see if you can get yourself invited to a Seder.

The Passover meal is long and drawn out, where the story of Passover is told before eating. However, unlike more solemn holidays, you are supposed to sit back, relax, and be as comfortable as possible while you partake (this is because free people have the luxury of lingering over a lavish meal). Luxuriate in the feast, and afterwards talk about what the two of you can do together to help people who are still oppressed.

ROMANTIC SIGN

ARIES (March 21st – April 20th)
Symbol: The Ram
Rules: The Head
Ruling Planet: Mars
Gem Stone: Ruby

Good Characteristics: self-starter, good initiative, gets things done, pioneering, straight-talker, a leader, loves romance, childlike, and adventurous.

Bad Characteristics: aggressive, a "me first" attitude, selfish, intolerant, reckless, arrogant, will sabotage anything, jealous, might cheat to get ahead.

Romantic Catch Phrase: "I'm so glad you wound up with me."

What it means: "You're so lucky to find me."

What it really means: "Thanks for putting up with me."

Most Romantic Thing You Can Say to an Aries: "You come first."

Top Ten Romantic Gifts for An Aries:

1. A head/scalp massage.
2. An appointment with the most expensive hairdresser or barber in town.
3. A personalized diary with pictures of him/her in it.
4. An antique mirror.
5. *The Art of War* by Lao Tzu.
6. *The Art of The Deal* by Donald Trump or anything by Donald Trump, including a weekend getaway to Mar-A-Lago, Trump's posh club in Palm Beach, Florida.
7. A handmade parchment scroll that lists "The Ten Things I Love About You."
8. A gorgeous fur hat or any kind of expensive hat.
9. A diamond tiara for a woman, a smoking jacket for a man.
10. Anything monogrammed or personalized with your lover's name on it.

African Astrology Symbol:

Community Leader (April 5th – May 4th)

Body Type: Strong and agile.

Personality Traits: Into community service, functions better in a group environment, cares about civic pride and well-being, good leader in politics, organizer.

Most Romantic Gift: A couple's sight-seeing trip anywhere.

Favorite Colors: Purples and yellows.

How To Win Their Heart Forever: Tell her how proud you are of her for all her wonderful acts of community service.

May

Memorial Day (last Monday in May)
This holiday officially marks the end of spring and the beginning of summer. Although most of us are thinking about the start of summer fun and sunshine, try not to forget the real meaning behind this all-American holiday. Good men and women gave their lives for us to live in freedom, so remember to do something patriotic (and romantic) during this long weekend. March in the Memorial Day Parade, or bring flags to wave and enjoy yourselves as spectators.

ROMANTIC SIGN

TAURUS (April 21st – May 21st)
Symbol: The Bull
Rules: The Throat, Face, and Eyes
Ruling Planet: Venus
Gem Stone: Emerald
Good Characteristics: productive, earthy, great in business, has endurance, slow to anger, loves food, money, and all creature comforts, very strong-willed and determined, very loyal, truthful, ambitious, usually in a good mood.
Bad Characteristics: stubborn, greedy, selfish, hordes things, possessive, boring, jealous, reactionary, self-indulgent.
Romantic Catch Phrase: "You taste so good."
What It Means: "I can't do anything until I get something to eat."
What It Really Means: "A romantic meal will put me in the mood for love."

Most Romantic Thing You Can Say to a Taurus: "Let's lock ourselves in the bedroom with whipped cream and hot fudge."

Top Ten Romantic Gifts for a Taurus:

1. A gourmet meal at the hottest restaurant in town.
2. A bag of chocolate money or candy dollar bills.
3. A new duvet.
4. A Lazy Boy recliner.
5. Breakfast, lunch, and dinner in bed.
6. Edible underwear and flavored body gels.
7. A weekend away at an inn famous for its large country breakfasts.
8. A lottery ticket.
9. Any book or video that tells you how to use food with sex.
10. French or Italian cooking lessons.

AFRICAN ASTROLOGY SYMBOL:

A Place For Shopping (May 5th – June 4th)
Body Type: Tall or short but always powerful looking.
Personality Traits: Interested in other people, powerful personality, wants to be a good provider, loving.
Most Romantic Gift: A gorgeous necklace.
Favorite Colors: Oranges and reds.
How To Win Their Heart Forever: Buy them a life insurance policy and give them fire-eating lessons.

Summer

SUMMER OF LOVE

Now we are about to enter into one of the most fun-filled, romantic times of year. With endless golden sunshine blazing in the blue sky above and the warming seas sparkling with inviting waves, lovers will find there is nothing as fantastic as a summer romance. This summer, make it your mission to recapture the romance in your life, whether that's keeping the flames of an established love burning brightly, or finding a new affair. You have no excuse. As long as you are living and breathing, summer naturally creates the perfect time to hit the beach and discover an ocean of love. Get out there and make it happen!

MONDAY–FRIDAY AROMATHERAPY

Sunday

Relaxation: Marjoram

Marjoram's calming effect can help put frightening thoughts into perspective. It is best used in small doses to take your troubles away.

Monday
Clarity: Clary Sage
Clary sage promotes expansiveness and clear thinking and helps lovers widen their horizons.

Tuesday
Balance: Basil
Basil can fortify a romance by helping each of you honor and respect your own identity first, giving you room to honor and respect your partner.

Wednesday
Healing: Tea Tree
Tea tree oil can clear up almost any type of skin irritation. It makes you feel crispy clean and ready to get closer to the one you love.

Thursday
Rejuvenation: Peppermint
Peppermint is a great uplifter. It can give new life to tired, achy muscles.

Friday
Passion: Jasmine
Jasmine is an exotic aphrodisiac that promotes extravagant fantasies, boundless creativity, and intensified perception.

Saturday
Play: Orange
Orange oil will make you feel light, friendly, and open. An orange oil massage can make you and your lover feel bright and sunny all over!

SUMMER ACTIVITIES

Rock and Roll Baby, Yeah!

Since the 1950s, rock and roll has been the music of love and romance. Any lover can tell you about a rock song that has a special romantic meaning to her. It doesn't matter which generation you and your lover grew up in, either. Whether it's Elvis, the Beatles, Simon and Garfunkel, Crosby, Stills, and Nash, the Police, or Britney Spears, American romances have been set to music by the rock and roll industry. So, this summer don't be afraid to splurge a little and buy those front row seats to a hot summer rock concert. Pop your lover up onto your shoulder, scream and shout, and let it out.

All's Fair in Summer Love

Another fun summertime romantic activity is to go to a county fair. Once again, you can relive your carefree childhood days as you take a trip into the Fun House, ride the upside-down roller coaster, and stuff your faces with cotton candy. Some local carnivals may offer "Midnight Madness," when you pay one price and ride all the rides you want from midnight to 4:00 AM. You and your lover will have a super time wearing yourselves out as you whip around on the Ferris wheel in the romantic moonlight.

If you and your lover are really into wild rides and junk food, why wait for a fair to come to town? Find out where the closest amusement park is and have yourselves a rip-roaring, exhilarating time.

Pull Over and Park It, Baby

OK, most of you reading this book probably have a proper place to make love like a bedroom, kitchen, living room, and so on. Wasn't it fun, though, when you were a teenager and had nowhere to go but the

back seat of your dad's car? Trying not to go "too far" in spite of those raging hormones combined with the thrill of maybe being caught made "making out" in the back seat a hot and heavy romantic interlude. Just for fun this summer, drive your car to the local "make-out" spot and relive those teen-dream years. If you don't have a "make-out" spot, or you are too "out-of-it" to know where it is, then find any safe, secluded area where you and your lover can have a good time.

Drive-By Romance

If, by chance, there is still a drive-in movie in your area, this is a perfect place for a romantic interlude.

Rent Summer of '42

This is one of the sexiest coming-of-age summer movies of all time. A young boy's loss of innocence, combined with the gorgeous, unspoiled Cape Cod scenery, creates a beautiful summer film that can be enjoyed again and again. This film will take you and your lover back to a simpler time when you could sleep in a beach cottage with the door open, and a strawberry ice cream cone cost three cents. It will also remind you how precious love and life are and to celebrate your romance every day you can. The haunting music in this film also makes a marvelous backdrop for passionate "rediscovery."

Take It Off

Because of the friendly weather, summer is an excellent time for outdoor naked activities. Here are a couple incredible things that you can do naked. Oh, how we love SUMMER!

1. The Nude Beach

Whether you and your lover fly off to the South of France or drive a couple of miles to a nearby nude beach, there is a simple way to add a bit of extra fun to sun-filled days. You and your lover will enjoy the uninhibited sense of freedom as you frolic shamelessly in the waves and bury more than your toes in the sand. Once you and your lover get over the initial Adam and Eve, "Oh my God, we're naked" response, then you will actually begin to feel amazingly relaxed and comfortable. Not only is going to a nude beach an exciting activity for you and your lover, but there is an extra perk: people watching takes on a whole new meaning.

2. Elysium Fields

For those of you lovers who really enjoyed your nude day at the beach, there's more summertime fun in store for you at a real nudist colony. Perhaps the most famous nudist colony in the country is Elysium Fields, located in Topanga Canyon in Malibu, California. However you don't have to go all the way out to Hollywierd to live the naturalist lifestyle. Check around your local area and you will find a place to go where Mother Nature's favorite outfit is always in style.

Summer Picnic

This summer why not stuff a picnic basket full of gourmet goodies, grab a bottle of wine, a big blanket, a CD player, and head outside for a romantic picnic? Find a secluded place in the woods or by a pond, or stay in your own backyard. Feed each other grapes, lie on the ground and look up at the sky, and toast your lovely partnership.

Water, Water Everywhere

Summer is a great time to go cascading down river while white-water rafting. Feel the cool water splash over you as you and your lover scream with sheer delight.

Roller Girl, I Love You!

Just like in the movie *Boogie Nights*, you too can be a sexy "roller-girl" like Heather Graham. There is something very hot about a woman

who is constantly on the move, in and out of view on a warm summer's day. Stick on roller blades or skates and roll around all day. Put on some knee-pads and a cool-looking helmet in case you hit the skids. See if you can both rollerblade across town for margaritas, then take a taxi back!

Surf's Up!

You can't talk about fun in the sun without mentioning one of America's favorite summer pastimes: surfing! From Frankie Avalon and Annette Funicello hitting the waves in California all those years ago, to the bawdy babes of *Baywatch*, romance runs high when the surf is up! Even if you and your lover are not exactly "Malibu Barbie and Ken," you can still grab a surfboard and make a valiant attempt at "hanging ten."

Muddy Waters Run Deep

Probably the best places in the world to take a mud bath are in Israel near the Dead Sea or at the spa in Monticatini in the Tuscan Mountains. However, if you can't make it to Middle East or Italy this summer, you and your lover can cover your bodies from head to toe in a marvelous mud mask that you can find at any beauty counter in a major department store. Take advantage of the summer weather, pull out some lounge chairs, and let the sun bake in the mud. Have a playful time washing each other off with a garden hose, then jump in a pool or shower.

The Wind Beneath My Wings

Another great romantic sport is wind surfing. Learning is half the fun, especially if you have a lover helping you to get up and grab hold of the sail. Wind-surfing is very romantic because the two of you will topple on top of each other again and again.

Sounds Fishy to Me

For a beautiful summertime experience, share the wonder and intimacy of diving in the deep blue sea. Have a great time doing the "Mermaid thing" way down deep, spinning and gliding in the weightless environment. If you don't want to deal with scuba equipment, then you and your lover can try snorkeling and enjoy the same salty sensations.

Airborne

Is it a bird? Is it a plane? No, it's the super-lovers parasailing high above the clear blue bay. Imagine, you and your lover side by side, floating through the air on a parasailer. What a romantic feeling of love and freedom as you and your lover kiss the clouds goodbye.

At the Ballet

This summer is a good time for you and your lover to expand your musical tastes and knowledge of dance. To cultivate culture during the heated months, bring your CD player out and set it up poolside. Put on some Mozart, Beethoven, Bach, Vivaldi, or any one of your classical favorites and jump in the pool. You and your lover can then have a good laugh as you try to dance through the water. For a real splash, get out of the pool, then join hands and run and jump in together trying to remain in a graceful position. Just make sure you head for the deep end!

Work Through the Burn

If you and your lover are the type who would rather get root canals than listen to classical music, then water aerobics may be more fun for you. You and your lover can "get physical" in the pool by putting on an aerobics tape or some high energy disco music. For the true aqua-athletes, try your hands at water polo.

Let's Go Coconuts

You and your lover can have a summertime tropical sensation in the privacy of your own backyard. Just make yourselves a few frozen Piña Coladas in the blender, put on some Jimmy Buffet or Bob Marley, and rub each other with coconut-scented suntan oil as you bask in the glow of the summer sunshine.

Vodka or Rum Watermelon

This sexy summer treat is something that this author discovered on a train from Switzerland to Rome. Just get yourselves a huge watermelon and a bottle of vodka or rum. Split the watermelon down the middle and pour the liquor all over it. Put the watermelon in the freezer for five to seven minutes or in the refrigerator for fifteen to twenty minutes. Then indulge. Needless to say, this is a very sensual, heady experience!

Swing Your Partner

Even if you live in a Park Avenue penthouse, an old-fashioned square dance at a lively summer barn dance is a romantic getaway. You two really owe it to yourselves to drink some freshly-squeezed lemonade and munch on some powdered sugar-covered fried dough as a blue grass country band brings down the house. Not only is square dancing a romantic American tradition, it will also help you get rid of stress or tension.

Barbecue Babe

Now that the weather's changed for the better, it's time to get outside and grill that killer rack of ribs you've been boasting about all spring. Invite friends and have everyone share their favorite summertime romantic stories. Provide plenty of napkins but no utensils—grill corn-on-the-cob, potato wedges, even pineapple slices, and eat everything with your fingers. No matter how you choose to do it, nothing beats a romantic summer barbecue spread.

Like a Rhinestone Cowboy

A summer rodeo has a certain magic all its own. Don a couple ten gallon hats, jeans, and big silver belt buckles, and grab some ice cold beers while you sit in the stands. After a night of "whooping and yelling," check out some late night rodeo country music parties. A night at the rodeo is always an all-American romantic time.

Cocktails, Anyone?

For the lovers with the utmost class and refinement (and big bank accounts), there is nothing more soothing than a summer sail on a luxury yacht. You don't have to own your own vessel because it is very easy to rent a fully-staffed boat. Treat yourselves right and bring along some caviar and champagne. After all, what's a yacht trip without the proper accoutrements? You and your lover will have an absolutely smashing time!

Sleep Under the Stars

This summer, have a warm weather adventure sleeping outside. Let the warm earth be your bed and the stars be your blanket as you rest peacefully after making love. You can roll out one large sleeping bag in your backyard, or camp out in a local park. If you live near a beach, see if it's legal to spend the night there, and fall asleep listening to lapping waves.

Go Greased Lightning!

Another summer movie classic that brings out the hopeless romantic in all of us is *Grease*. This bubble-gum coming-of-age musical, starring

Olivia Newton John and a very young, handsome John Travolta, will make hearts of any age go pitter-patter.

Bowling

Bowling is making a major comeback! Summer is the perfect time for you and your lover to get the ball rolling. Invite another couple, grab some pizza and beer, and enjoy this simple pleasure. It may surprise you how much fun bowling really is. Before you know it, you'll have matching shirts, balls, and "lucky shoes." This is a fun, romantic night out, you and your lover will never outgrow.

Be Cool, Play Pool

If you and your lover want an easy, laid-back evening, but feel the need to get off the couch, then head down to the local pool hall and take turns getting behind the eight ball. Play your favorite songs on the jukebox, enjoy a couple of beers, and know that in the mysterious environment of a pool hall, you two are too cool for words!

Get Your Motor Running

Summer is a great time to hop on a Harley and head cross-country. Just make sure you keep your helmet on when you're speeding down the open road. To get the full experience, stop at a biker bar for a little lunch and tattoo-watching. You might find yourselves inscribing your names on each other's forearms (or on any other body parts)!

A Midsummer Night's Dream

This classic Shakespeare play is a sheer joy to watch, summer after summer. Check your local paper for a theater company with a performance at an outdoor theater. If either or both of you has caught the acting bug, then audition to perform in the production. Or, at least read the play together before you see it performed. You will be surprised how romantic it is to read Shakespeare's eternal words to each other as you rehearse for the big opening night.

ROMANTIC SUMMER HOLIDAYS

Summer is such a gorgeous season for romance, it's a shame there are so few holidays in June, July, and August. However, that shouldn't stop you and your lover from celebrating romance. Below are some suggestions on how to be romantic during the traditional holidays as well as some made-up holidays to enjoy.

MADE-UP ROMANTIC SUMMER HOLIDAYS

Favorite Color Day

Pick a day when you touch everything in your lover's world with their favorite color. If their favorite color is red:

❧ Buy them a red tie or scarf, baseball hat, or any article of clothing.

❧ Buy yourself a new red outfit.

❧ Put red soap or bath gel in the shower or draw a romantic bath with red bath salts.

❧ Make a red dessert like cherry pie, strawberry sorbet, jello, or cake with red icing.

❧ Put together a little gift with all of their favorite red things (such as candy, toys, a flower, new undies, etc.).

❧ Go online and find out everything you can about the color red—what mood it represents, what it symbolized in ancient civilizations, what countries have it in their flag and why. Then make a chart or painting using your information.

❧ Buy or make a piece of jewelry featuring rubies, garnets, or red glass beads or enamel.

❧ Write a poem or a paragraph about why you think he loves red and what qualities it represents.

❧ Send a red plant or flowers to the office.

❧ Put a red sticker that says "I love you" on each of his CD covers.

Favorite Music Day

Fill your lover's day with his favorite sounds. Here are a few suggestions using Led Zeppelin as an example:

❧ Buy every album ever made by this group that he or she doesn't already have.

❧ Call your local record store or go online to see if there are any rough cuts from a live concert available.

❧ If the band is currently on tour, buy front row seats to an out-of-town concert and plan a whole romantic weekend around it.

❧ Instead of the alarm clock, wake him up with Led Zeppelin.

❧ Place a Led Zeppelin CD in the car CD player in the morning.

❧ Call a radio station and dedicate a Led Zeppelin song to your lover.

❧ Go to a place with a karaoke machine and bring along a tape recorder. Record yourself singing his favorite Led Zeppelin songs.

❧ Get a classic Led Zeppelin T-shirt and concert posters. Be wearing the T-shirt and nothing else when he comes home.

❧ Go on www.ebay.com and see if there is any incredible Led Zeppelin paraphernalia being auctioned off.

Favorite Food Day

Is there a food your lover just can't get enough of? Indulge her by making sure she gets it all day. Don't be afraid to get creative! Here are some ideas using pizza and lobster as examples:

❧ For breakfast, serve smoked salmon and caviar pizza, or lobster puffs. To make the pizza, just smear cream cheese on a tortilla or pita bread and top with smoked salmon and a dab of caviar. To make lobster puffs, cut up little bits of lobster and bake them into some "Pop and Fresh" dough or any type of quick biscuits.

❧ Pack her a snack of Wolfgang Puck barbecued chicken pizza (in your grocer's freezer) and a chilled lobster cocktail on ice.

❧ Show up at their office with a clambake, lobster salad sandwiches, or pizza for lunch. If you really want to make an impression, bring enough for the whole office.

❧ Take her out for lunch to a fancy restaurant that specializes in Lobster Thermidor.

- Surprise her for dinner with a "make-your-own-pizza" night. Use frozen dough, or have a blast making it from scratch, especially when you flip the dough up in the air! Have lots of different toppings ready and make one large mosaic pizza, or small individual pizzas.

- Order in a large pizza and spell out "I love you _____" using black olives, onions, or peppers to spell out her name.

- Get some fresh live lobsters and have a great time cooking them together.

- Make a "cookies and ice cream pizza" for dessert. Just get one huge chocolate chip cookie and pile your favorite flavors of ice cream, fudge, butterscotch, and nuts on top.

Favorite Movie Day

Create a "life in your favorite movie" day and let your lover live out their film fantasies. Here are some suggestions using the film *Animal House*.

- Have a spontaneous food fight.

- Dress up as a virgin sorority girl or new pledge.

- Have a toga party.

- If your lover lived in a fraternity or sorority house in college, find its picture in his or her yearbook and have it blown up to poster size. Write "Animal House" underneath and have it framed.

🖤 Invite a favorite Greek buddy whom he hasn't seen in a long time to call or come for a surprise visit.

🖤 Tell her she's being romantically "hazed" and must do three romantic things of your choice before you let her into your "Fraternity Of Love."

"This Is Your Life" Day

If you do a little homework first, this can truly be a day to remember. Here are some ideas on how to make your lover feel special from morning 'til night.

🖤 Call his parents and ask for baby pictures and home movies. Create a huge montage and make sure it is the first thing he sees on waking up in the morning. Play movies of his childhood in the background.

🖤 Find out what her favorite breakfast was as a kid and have it ready.

🖤 Find an old grade-school friend and have him call before your lover goes to work.

🖤 Get a CD of her favorite music from high school and put it in the car CD player.

🖤 If he was on a sports team in high school, get an old uniform, team photos and trophies and send them to the office. You can send a prom picture, also.

🖤 Have her high school coach or prom date call her at work.

◈ Look through his yearbook for the names of all his friends who signed it. See if you can locate them. Ask each one of them for a current photo and a letter about what is going on their lives right now. Make an "updated yearbook" with all their letters and current pictures.

◈ If she had a Bat Mitzvah or Confirmation, have the priest or rabbi who did the ceremony call or write a letter.

◈ Ask his parents if they have any of your lover's old toys—or something important to him as a kid, like a bicycle—and borrow them to put all around the house.

◈ Buy her the same type of pet she had as a child.

◈ Throw a surprise party with all the people who called during the day and anyone else who would qualify as a "blast from the past." Serve only his favorite foods and drinks. Ask everyone to use your lover's old nickname.

◈ End the day by reading a poem about why she is so important to you and why she is the best lover in the whole world!

Favorite Hobby Day

Most people don't have enough time in their busy schedules to do what they love often enough. On this day, make sure your lover gets plenty of time and support to indulge his or her passion. Below are some ideas using tennis as an example:

◈ Schedule an early morning game before work or a late afternoon game when he comes home.

- Set up a lesson with a famous pro in your area.

- Buy a membership to an exclusive tennis club in your area.

- Give him a stack of tennis videos, a new racquet, or a ball machine so he can practice.

- Enter him in a "round robin" so he always has a game scheduled.

- Learn to play the game better yourself, so you can spend more time together sharing a favorite hobby.

- Buy him some new tennis clothes.

- Plan a surprise trip to Wimbledon or the U.S. Open.

- Get him an autographed picture of a favorite tennis star.

- Suggest he starts an "office" tennis team.

- Buy a weekend at an exclusive tennis clinic. Make sure you're there, too!

Favorite Animal Day

Use your creativity to help your lover connect with their inner beast. Fill the day with reminders of a favorite pet or a favorite wild animal. For instance, if she's wild about lions:

- Have a picnic lunch at the local zoo and watch the lions being fed.

- Take her to a circus or a Lion Country Safari Park.

❧ Start planning a trip to Africa for a real safari.

❧ Buy her a copy of *Born Free*.

❧ Give her a list of ten qualities that she shares with a lion.

❧ Go out and buy the biggest stuffed animal lion you can find.

❧ Find out what the lion symbolizes in other cultures and ancient religions.

❧ Call the local zoo and see if you can "adopt" a lion or even feed a cub.

❧ Join a charity that protects lions and other jungle wildlife like the MasiMara Foundation or World Wildlife Fund.

Favorite Movie Star Day

If your lover has a celluloid someone they adore, here's how to bring their idol right into your own living room.

❧ Call up the *National Enquirer* or the *Star* and ask them to send you a clip of every story written on the actor in the last year. Both papers have offices in Los Angeles, California.

❧ Call the Screen Actors' Guild in Hollywood, and find out who the actor's publicist is. Call the publicist and fax a written request for an autographed picture.

❧ Buy videos or DVDs of all their movies.

❧ Get a cheap copy of the favorite's Oscar night garb (most department stores carry this after the Oscars) and wear it for your own Oscar night.

✿ Find out the actor's hometown and get some memorabilia from there.

✿ Call the Drama Book Store in Los Angeles, and see if you can buy a script from their last movie.

✿ Go on www.ebay.com and see if the actor is involved in any celebrity charity auctions. Buy your lover something that his favorite is auctioning off.

✿ Sign up for the actor's fan club.

✿ Give your lover a list of ten things he has in common with his favorite star, such as personality traits, physical characteristics, likes, and dislikes. (The *Star*, *Globe* or *National Enquirer* can be excellent sources for this kind of info.)

Favorite Book Day

Show your lover how much you respect her appreciation of a favorite book or author. For instance, if she loves all things to do with Shakespeare:

✿ Wake her up with a few romantic lines from *Romeo and Juliet*.

✿ Write a quote from a Shakespeare love sonnet or play in shaving cream on the bathroom mirror.

✿ Role play two favorite Shakespearean lovers. Call each other "Titania" and "Oberon" or "Romeo" and "Juliet" all day.

✿ Prepare an old English feast for dinner.

- Write a list of qualities she has in common with her favorite Shakespearean character.

- Surprise her with tickets to London to see a production at the Old Globe Theater and a day trip to Stratford-Upon-Avon, Shakespeare's birthplace.

- Write your own love sonnet using Shakespearean language.

- Spend the evening analyzing a favorite work of Shakespeare and discussing its new meaning for today.

- Invite a group of friends for an evening of Shakespeare. Give everyone a copy of your lover's favorite play and take turns reading aloud.

Fantasy Job Day

Is your lover an accountant who wants to be an artist? Or a doctor who always wanted to be a rock star? Give your lover the chance to recapture their favorite fantasy. Here are some suggestions using "rock star" as an example:

- Get a karaoke machine with his favorite rock band's songs on it and let him perform to his heart's content.

- Suggest he gets an outrageous, rock and roll, heavy metal hairdo.

- Get a few willing friends to form an "air guitar" band and spend the afternoon jamming out his favorite rock band's songs.

- Give him some wild and crazy, rock and roll leather outfits, or T-shirts with his favorite band on it.

- Throw a "rock and roll" evening of debauchery with loud music and friends who love the rock scene.

- If he plays an instrument, encourage him to start practicing again on a regular basis. Set up your garage or basement as a place for him to practice.

- Call local nightclubs and ask if they know a band that is holding auditions. Encourage your lover to try out.

- Call a local radio station and ask how to get backstage passes for a performance by his favorite group.

- Give him a list of ten reasons why it's a good thing he didn't actually become a rock star.

Favorite Decade Day

Do you have a lover who you could swear is reincarnated from a different time period? Give your lover a day in that era when her soul feels most at home. Here are some suggestions using the 1960s as an example:

- Have a love-in at your house.

- Take down the door to the bedroom and put up a bead curtain.

- Tie-dye everything.

- Paint a peace sign on everything.

❧ Get a video of JFK's "Ask not what your country can do for you, but what you can do for your country" speech.

❧ Borrow or rent an old van and have a party in it.

❧ Buy and listen to a tape of the original Woodstock Live Concert.

❧ Get tickets to a "Beatle Mania" performance near you.

❧ Rent the movie *Hair*.

❧ Visit the Height-Ashbury section of San Francisco.

Summer Camp Day

Return to those happy-go-lucky summertime days by turning your home into a summer camp. Here are some suggestions on how to take your lover on this trip down memory lane:

❧ Get out her camp yearbook or group photo and display it on the breakfast table.

❧ Short-sheet her bed.

❧ Regale her with old camp songs. Encourage her to sing along.

❧ Find out if her camp had a "color war" and decorate the whole house in her team's color.

❧ Send her a "care package" full of toilet paper, candy, and comic books.

- If the camp is still in business, take a reunion trip and see what it is like today.

- Get her to tell you her most painful camp story, then rewrite it with a happy ending.

- Pretend you are the counselor she had a crush on and seduce her in a secluded, woodsy spot.

- Make her favorite camp food.

- Do her favorite camp activity.

- Invite some friends over and make up goofy skits.

- Find a lake and cannonball in.

- Do arts and crafts indoors if it's a rainy day.

- If she was a counselor, pretend that you are a homesick "unhappy camper" and run to her arms for comfort.

Favorite Season Day

Just because it's summer, you don't have to have all sunshine and beach days. Re-create your lover's favorite season (or next favorite, if he or she likes summer best). Who says it can't snow on the Fourth or July! Here are some ways to beat the hot summertime blues, if winter is a favorite:

- Turn your air conditioning down to 50 degrees.

- Walk around your super-air-conditioned house in your winter coats.

- Find an indoor ice skating rink that is open year 'round.

- Visit Australia, New Zealand, or parts of South America. Our summer is their winter.

- Visit the Swiss Alps—the Swiss always have snow on the mountaintops.

- Have a "Five Months 'til Christmas Party" in July. Hang stockings, exchange presents, play Christmas music, dress up as Santa, and make a big dinner.

- Go to an indoor "ski-dome."

- Start a fire in your fireplace.

ROMANTIC SUMMER HOT SPOTS

During the summer there is a myriad of places all over the world to choose from. Here is a close-up look at three of the most romantic summer destinations.

The Hamptons: A Summer's Guide to a Rich and Famous Romance

Perhaps the most famous place in the United States to spend your summer break is in the Hamptons. Located on the eastern section of Long Island, the Hamptons are often referred to as New York's Riviera. This is because they attract celebrities, Wall Streeters, music business entrepreneurs, trend-setting designers, everyone and anyone who is somehow involved in the world of chic style. People from all over the United States and Europe visit these quaint little hamlets when they want some real summer excitement. However, what a lot of people don't know is that there is another side to the Hamptons which is down to earth and very romantic in a "beachy" laid-back way. Whether you and your lover choose to make a big splash on the high-profile celebrity scene, or just prefer to play it cool by the pool, the two of you can have the time of your lives in this very unique country setting. Below are some suggestions on how to make the most of the best romantic scenarios the Hamptons have to offer summer lovers.

1. People Watching at the Barefoot Contessa or Loaves and Fishes

You will find more at these gourmet havens than just giant brioches and a selection of French cheeses. Since the Hamptons tries its best to have a casual and relaxed atmosphere, most celebrities and famous folk feel quite comfortable popping into the local food store to pick up their flavored coffee and artichoke dip. You never know who you and your lover might meet at the deli counter or see blowing their diet at the irresistible bakery. So put on your shorts and baseball caps, and try to look nonchalant when you spy on celebs as they shop for chow.

2. Clubbing

After a day at the pool, life begins at night in the Hamptons with its star-studded club scene. Every year the clubs change names and venues, but there are some places that never go out of style. At Stephen's Talk House in Amagansett, you and your lover could very well be there when local stars drop in for an impromptu jam session. If you are going to the Talk House, throw on an old pair of shorts, t-shirts, and flip flops and leave your diamonds and pearls at home. This is one place where Hamptons' pretension is checked at the door. However, if you

and your lover would rather dance the night away to a disco beat behind the velvet rope in the V.I.P. section, then grab a limo over to Conscious Point or the Tavern. These two nightclubs promise a happening scene every year.

3. Taste of the Hamptons

Every summer, all the local restaurants and wineries put on a food festival that can't be beat. For one entry price, you and your lover can sample delicious delicacies from every restaurant for which you'd normally wait a month to get a reservation. This gastronomic gala takes place in a big open field under a tent, so you'll never feel you have to fight the crowds to get some lobster ceviche or warm apple pie with fresh whipped cream. There's always a good band for dancing off all the calories you two ingested earlier in the evening.

4. Sunrise at Montauk Point or Gosman's Marina

When you and your lover eventually tire of all the Hamptons flash and spending, then it will be time to enjoy the simpler joys this area has to offer. Forgo the club hopping one night, set an early alarm clock, and head east out to Montauk Point to see the sunrise. You and your lover will experience true peace and tranquillity as you gaze out over this natural harbor. Around lunchtime, wander over to Gosman's Marina for some of the freshest seafood you will ever eat. Hamptons locals know that the secret to good summer living is mixing the high life with some much needed back-to-basics enjoyment.

5. Ocean Mansion Fantasy

If you dream of dwelling in a palace by the sea, but your budget won't let you do that (yet!), then you and your lover can have a fantastic bike ride along Dune Road, viewing some of the most magnificent stately homes you will ever see. After a ride like that, you may find yourselves motivated to start that new business, or at least buy a bunch of lottery tickets!

6. Sag Harbor

Sag Harbor is one of the most romantic areas in the Hamptons. Once an old whaling village, Sag Harbor is filled with romantic "haunted" mansions and former Captain's homes. Spend an afternoon hearing local folklore and historic tales of the sea. When you are ready to re-enter the twenty-first century, Sag Harbor has wonderful antique shops, galleries, homemade ice cream, bars, and wonderful restaurants on the pier. Enjoy the sunset over the Sag Harbor Bridge, as you and lover sip a cocktail and watch the yachts go by.

7. Give Me Shelter

If you and your lover really want to get away from it all, Shelter Island is the Hamptons' answer to serenity and privacy. The only way to get to this secluded spot is by ferry. You will feel like landed gentry on your own island in the middle of the Long Island Sound. The rolling hills and wooded paths will make you feel worlds away from everything. Even though the whole area is filled with the rich and famous, the REALLY rich and famous who want to escape the intrusive paparazzi and Hamptons summer hubbub sail peacefully away to Shelter Island.

8. Penny Candy

A visit to the Penny Candy store in Water Mill (between Bridgehampton and Southampton) is an instant trip down memory lane. You and your lover can stuff your faces with favorites from your childhood days like Gob-Stoppers, Fireballs, Lemon Drops, Circus Peanuts, Pixie Sticks, and homemade fudge. Forget the diet and the dentist and fill up a big bag so you two can misbehave later. Kick off your shoes and head down to the beach to a full-on sweet and salty sensation.

9. Be a Classic

Every social summer season ends with The Hampton Classic Horse Show, held in Bridgehampton. This equestrian festival is

much more than a few ponies running and jumping over fences. There are a menagerie of chic shops, a petting zoo, exotic foods, and outdoor entertainment. On the final Sunday of the week-long event is the Grand Prix. Horses and riders compete for hundreds of thousands of dollars while members of the Hamptons' social set compete for prime seating under the exclusive owner's marquis. Whether you two rent some horses to ride in the Classic or sip something soothing on the sidelines, you simply cannot spend a summer in the Hamptons without popping over to the show grounds for this traditional romantic event.

London, England: Have Yourself a Royal Romance

Although merry old England will never win accolades for its weather, you can have so much fun there during the month of June that you will hardly notice the drizzle. During the last few weeks of June, London is alive with three of its most social events: Royal Ascot (the horse races), Henley (the regatta or sailboat races), and Wimbledon (the professional tennis match played on grass courts). All three of these events attract royalty, celebrities, and sports fans from around the world. Whether you are sitting way up in the bleachers downing a pint of lager at Wimbledon, watching the ships sail in at Henley, or observing the Queen inspect her fillies in Ascot's royal paddock, you and your lover are bound to have a blast of British fun. First time travelers to the U.K. should note that none of these sporting events resemble their American counterparts. They all have a style that is unique to the country that gave us Charles and Camilla and many other royal romantic dramas. Just for laughs, here is a beginner's guide to attending Royal Ascot. Cheerio!

1. Get into the Royal Enclosure

Believe it or not, rubbing shoulders with the Queen and her entourage is not as difficult as you might think at Royal Ascot. All you have to do is snag tickets to the Royal Enclosure and you will find yourselves sipping champagne and eating strawberries with the Lords and Ladies. Guess what? You don't have to have blue blood to mingle with the best of Britain. All you have to do is write a letter to the American Embassy in Britain and ask about the procedure for tickets into the Royal Enclosure. You don't need a king's ransom to do this either, because it is surprisingly affordable. Before you know it, you and your lover could be the talk of the afternoon.

2. Brown Bag It? Not Exactly!

Whether you make it into the Royal Enclosure or not, you and your lover can still follow the English tradition of having a picnic "hamper" out of the "boot" (trunk) of your car. There are no parking lots at Ascot, only large green fields that are perfect for setting up. When you arrive at Ascot, you will find that everyone who's anyone is putting out exquisitely catered lunches on folding tables under large umbrellas. It is quite a sight to see people in such formal attire eating out of the back of their cars, even if it is an Ascot tradition. A day or so before Ascot, simply phone up Fortnum & Mason on Piccadilly Road and tell them you need a romantic Ascot hamper made for two. You will be destined to find true love somewhere beneath a big glob of Devonshire cream and scones. Absolutely brilliant!

3. Win, Place, or Show

With all the food, fashion, and fanfare, don't forget that underneath it all, Ascot is a horse race! After watching the ponies parade around the royal paddock, why not place a few pounds (sterling) on your favorite horse? Who knows? You and your lover might win enough to buy yourselves an English country estate.

4. Ascot Balls

During the week of Ascot, many aristocrats throw balls in honor of the occasion. If you don't happen to have a Marquis, Duke, or

Duchess as your best buddy, you still can wangle your way into a great invite, once again by checking with the American Embassy. For the right price, we commoners can prance with a prince or dine and dance with a duke!

Monte Carlo, Monaco: The Ultimate Romantic Fairy Tale

Nestled high in the rocky hills above the calm Mediterranean Sea, lies the tiny principality of Monaco, perhaps one of the most romantic spots on earth. August is the perfect time to discover the magic of Monte Carlo. This is where a dashing Prince Rainier swept a young Grace Kelly off her feet in the glamorous 1950s. Here you'll find a fairy tale setting for lovers around the world to enjoy. No matter what your budget is, you can always find something romantic to experience in Monte Carlo. Here are some highlights that can help you live the dream…only in Monte Carlo.

1. The Red Cross Ball

Every year the top event of the summer is the International Red Cross Ball. Hosted by the first family of Monaco, this ball is a chance to glance at and dance with the crème de la crème of European society. You're sure to be dazzled by the millions of dollars' worth of astounding jewelry. Even if you and your lover are getting room service and skipping the ball, pop on over to the bar at the Hotel De Paris, where everyone goes for a drink before the main event at the Monte Carlo Sporting Club.

2. Reach the Beach

The Monte Carlo Beach Club is the place to be seen by the *piscine* (French for pool) either topless or wearing your teeny tiniest bikini. Walk hand in hand down the rocky shoreline or sneak off into a private cabana for a little afternoon delight.

3. Place Your Bets

The Monte Carlo Casino was once the grand dame of international gambling. Even though its heyday has past, you can still place your bets at any one of the gaming tables and slot machines. The building itself is one of grand romantic splendor that will transport you and your lover to a time gone by.

4. Get Grilled

The Grill Room on top of the Hotel De Paris is the epitome of a romantic place to share a quiet dinner. On a clear night, they open the rooftop, so that you and your lover are covered by a blanket of stars.

5. Go Above it All

Enjoy the staggering cliffs and gorgeous palaces from an aerial view by taking a helicopter ride along the coast. Nowhere on Earth will you be able to take in such magnificent opulence as you glide in the clouds. The Hotel De Paris and Hotel Hermitage offer complimentary helicopter transport from the Nice Airport to the Monte Carlo landing pad. Take advantage of this wonderful service and get a "high-in-the sky" start to your magical Monte Carlo romance.

6. Yachting, Anyone?

One of the most privileged ways to enjoy Monte Carlo is by staying aboard a private yacht. You can't help but fall in love on one of Monte Carlo's vessels of love! If vacationing on a yacht is not in your budget, then get in touch with your hotel's concierge or the Monte Carlo Harbormaster to see about available day cruises. While sailing aimlessly around this Mediterranean paradise, you and your lover can feel like royalty even on a "Cinderella" budget.

June

Summer Solstice (June 21st)

One extremely romantic way of welcoming in the first day of summer is by spending the night making love on the beach. You and your lover will be tempted to spill your deepest secrets as the warm flames flicker in the summer moonlight. A sandy beach bonfire also makes the perfect setting for a marriage proposal or even a "let's move in together" proposition.

ROMANTIC SIGN

GEMINI (May 22nd – June 21st)

Symbol: The Twins

Rules: Arms, Ears, Nose

Ruling Planet: Mercury

Gem Stone: Rock Crystal

Good Characteristics: quick thinking, inventive, great with hands, adaptable, loves anything to do with the mind, trendy, good speaker, adventurous, makes friends, and looks good.

Bad Characteristics: restless, two-faced, can't be trusted, fickle, nervous, flirtatious, too smart for their own good, talks their way out of trouble, changes mind quickly.

Romantic Catch Phrase: "It seems like a good idea that we are together."

What it means: "I like being with you for now."

What it really means: "I know this is a good thing, so I'm trying not to mess it up."

Most Romantic Thing You Can Say to a Gemini: "With you, everyday is different and exciting."

Top Ten Gifts for a Gemini:
1. Fur ear muffs.
2. A new computer game.
3. A VIP pass to the hottest nightclub in town.
4. A getaway where you do something different every day.
5. A new outfit or pair of shoes that reflect the latest winter fashion.
6. A winter membership to the gym.
7. A different tie or scarf for every day of the week.
8. A trip to a new city.
9. A diamond studded earring.
10. A temporary tattoo kit.

AFRICAN ASTROLOGY SYMBOL:

The Elder or the Ancestor (June 5th – July 4th)
Body Type: Tall, proud, and stately.
Personality Traits: Born to rule, very fair, understands the needs of others, regal, and knowledgeable.
Most Romantic Gift: A distinguished smoking jacket.
Favorite Colors: Rich reds.
How To Win Their Heart Forever: Say, "You're a wise old soul with a gorgeous young face and heart."

July

Canada Day (July 1st)

Why not help our Northern neighbors celebrate their national holiday by visiting their beautiful country? Even though Canada is right next door, many Americans have never been there. Have a blast checking out the romantic potential of Toronto, Quebec, and Montreal, as well as the natural beauty of the vast countryside. Canada has the romantic charm of European culture without being a world away. If you can't get to Canada this summer, hang a Canadian flag, drink some Canadian Club, and make love while listening to Celine Dion.

Independence Day (July 4th)

Independence Day is one of the most fun, romantic days of summer. You'll want to catch as many fireworks as you can (check your local paper for schedules for the towns near you). Many towns have pops music festivals over July 4th weekend. Bring a picnic and a blanket and take in a concert, lolling around in the cool of the evening listening to pops music. If you and your lover want to make your own fireworks this year, buy some sparklers and celebrate with champagne and strawberries, blueberries, and whipped cream (red, white and blue!)

ROMANTIC SIGN

CANCER (June 22nd –July 22nd)

Symbol: The Crab
Rules: Heart, Chest

Ruling Planet: The Moon

Gem Stone: Moon Stone

Good Characteristics: love of home and family, good parent and caretaker, imaginative, supportive, protective, loyal, nurturer, kind, emotional, loving.

Bad Characteristics: moody, penny pincher, needy, clingy, overly emotional, martyr, can choose unhealthy friends or lovers, worrier, self-pity.

Romantic Catch Phrase: "You remind me of my mom (or dad)."

What It Means: "I am comfortable with you."

What it Really Means: "Maybe I could marry you."

Most Romantic Thing You Can Say to a Cancer: "I feel so loved and protected when I cuddle up with you."

Top Ten Gifts for a Cancer:

1. A family album.
2. A certificate to a company or a website that traces his/her family tree.
3. A magazine or book that shows how to redecorate or add on to your home.
4. A trip to see a relative who lives far away.
5. A handmade parchment scroll that lists "100 Reasons Why I Will Never Leave You."
6. A book of children's names.
7. A trip to the country of his/her ethnic heritage.
8. Take her shopping for a new home.
9. A mood ring.
10. An artist's easel or drawing board.

AFRICAN ASTROLOGY SYMBOL:

The Young Woman (July 5th – August 4th)
Body Type: Thin and wiry, may have freckles and pink skin.
Personality Traits: Youthful, enthusiastic, bright, smiling, laughs a lot, loves practical jokes and having fun.
Most Romantic Gift: A gift certificate or shopping spree.
Favorite Colors: Pastel pink and baby blues.
How To Win Their Heart Forever: Be light, fun, gossipy, and don't forget to giggle a lot.

August

ROMANTIC SIGN

LEO (July 23rd – August 23rd)
Symbol: The Lion
Rules: Stomach
Ruling Planet: The Sun
Gem Stone: Tiger's Eye
Good Characteristics: dignified, honorable, sunny disposition, leader, romantic, capable of great love, good self-promoter.
Bad Characteristics: too much entitlement, arrogant, self-centered, pompous, too much self-importance, can put career over everything else.
Romantic Catch Phrase: "I am having a great love affair!"
What It Means: "Everything I do, I do in a big way."
What It Really Means: "You are the sunshine of my life."
Most Romantic Thing You Can Say to a Leo: "Basking in your glory keeps me warm."

Top Ten Gifts for a Leo:

1. A trip to Miami or any sunny climate.
2. A tanning bed.
3. An expensive self-tanning gift set.
4. A book of European royalty and castles.
5. Biographies of the world's most famous leaders.
6. Biographies of the world's most famous celebrities.
7. A handmade parchment scroll that lists "Why I Think You Could Rule The World."

8. Hire an artist to paint a portrait of your lover in a regal looking outfit.
9. A big gold chain.
10. Anything that says "You Are The King Of My Heart" on it.

AFRICAN ASTROLOGY SYMBOL:

A Hard Shelled Nut (August 5th – September 3rd)
Body Type: Plump, meaty, or round.
Personality Traits: Sexy, lust and live for love, good intuition, free and energetic, loves to have a good time.
Most Romantic Gift: Edible undies.
Favorite Colors: Gold and silver.
How To Win Their Heart Forever: Feed and make love to them all day and all night.

365 Quickies

1. Leave a rose on the breakfast table.
2. Feed the swans together on a fresh spring day.
3. Surprise your lover in the shower.
4. Put a cup of hot coffee in the car's drink holder with a donut. Write "I love you" on the napkin.
5. Go to Paris.
6. Take out a classified ad affirming your love.
7. Sing a love song.
8. Hire a harpist to serenade you.
9. Help each other climb a tree.
10. Rent a convertible. Kiss in the back seat.
11. Have a professional photographer shoot a romantic photo of the two of you.
12. Buy each other gift certificates.
13. Feed each other strawberries.
14. Write a valentine on the windshield.
15. Feed each other champagne.
16. Make up new nicknames.
17. Get a personalized bumper sticker that says "I love (name here)."
18. Cook brunch together.
19. Write your names in the sand.
20. Make origami.
21. Get monogrammed pillowcases with both your initials on them.
22. Buy satin sheets.

23. Make banana splits for each other.

24. Pamper each other.

25. Serve a sexy dessert wine with a simple meal.

26. Frame both your baby pictures together.

27. Roller skate together.

28. Adopt a tree in your neighborhood. Visit every day.

29. Bake each other a cake.

30. Feed each other M&M's.

31. Book a romantic weekend getaway.

32. Kiss your lover's eyebrows.

33. Assign each other a "personal gemstone."

34. Wade down a stream. Look under the rocks.

35. Work in the yard together.

36. Trace each other's family trees.

37. Buy two love birds, and name them after each other.

38. Leave a bag of Hershey's kisses on the dashboard.

39. Have a single rose delivered to your lover's workplace.

40. Hold hands everywhere you go.

41. Kiss for at least fifteen seconds in the morning.

42. Kiss for at least fifteen seconds when you first see each other after work.

43. Wash the windows together.

44. Go to the movies.

45. Stay home and make popcorn.

46. Eat out at the most expensive restaurant in town.

47. Dine in on leftovers by candlelight.

48. Go to a live theater production.

49. Look at some art.

50. Eat a bag lunch on a boardwalk.

51. Take a road trip.

52. Misbehave while waiting for a table in a restaurant.

53. Leave a big tip.

54. Feed each other chocolates.

55. Buy something extravagant.

56. Play outside.

57. Watch *A Star Is Born* together.

58. Watch *Notting Hill* together.

59. Watch *Sleepless In Seattle* together.

60. Exchange gifts.

61. Get a sky writer to write your names in the sky.

62. Share an umbrella.

63. Get dressed up.

64. Go casual.

65. Buy balloons.

66. Read celebrity gossip together.

67. Shop for curtains.

68. Do something unexpected.

69. Wear your oldest sweats and cuddle up on the couch.

70. Walk in the rain.

71. Get away from it all.

72. See how far you can walk while holding hands.

73. Ride in a limousine.

74. Share an ice cream cone.

75. Read the story of the Taj Mahal. Plan to visit.

76. Watch a nature video.

77. Look your lover straight in the eyes and say, "I love you."

78. Fill the bedroom with flowers.

79. Try a little role playing.

80. Wear as little as possible.

81. Go on a wilderness vacation together.

82. Play hide & seek.

83. Whisper sweet nothings.

84. Have a candlelit dinner on the roof of a tall building.
85. Have a hot dog eating contest.
86. Feed each other french fries.
87. Take turns reading aloud to each other in bed.
88. Have your lover's favorite lunch delivered to her workplace.
89. Splurge!
90. Plant a garden together.
91. Plan your dream house together.
92. Go to a U-Pick farm and pick strawberries.
93. Paddle a canoe together. Fall in.
94. Go to an outdoor wine tasting.
95. Have your portraits painted.
96. Build a sandcastle.
97. Get a bicycle built for two.
98. Pick vegetables together.
99. Make each other straw hats.
100. Leave a rose in the shower.
101. Wear matching golf shorts.
102. Ask a stranger to take a picture of the two of you.
103. Play catch.
104. Have dinner along the banks of a river.
105. Look your lover straight in the eyes and say, "Thank you."
106. Nibble on your lover's earlobes.
107. Chase the ice cream truck on your bikes until the driver stops.
108. Buy all the neighborhood kids ice cream.
109. Rent *Tom Jones* and watch the sexy Inn scene.
110. Make a sexy video.
111. Learn a new sport together.
112. Wash the car together by hand. Get wet.
113. Feed each other honey off a spoon.
114. Ride bareback on the beach.

115. Cuddle in a hammock.

116. Play tag in a sunny meadow.

117. Rest!

118. Walk in the park.

119. Go window shopping.

120. Take a train ride.

121. Go barefoot.

122. Visit a travel agent and choose an exotic destination.

123. Surf the Web together.

124. Go to *The Rocky Horror Picture Show* together (bring squirt guns, newspaper, and toast—trust me).

125. Feed each other breakfast.

126. Brush each other's hair.

127. Go on a treasure hunt.

128. Shop for shoes.

129. Spend an hour at the Sharper Image playing with the massage toys.

130. Leave a rose in the car seat.

131. Giggle.

132. Roll in the mud.

133. Hose each other down.

134. Let a street artist paint or draw a portrait of the two of you.

135. Feed the ducks.

136. Make love in broad daylight.

137. Splash in the surf.

138. Go to a drive-in.

139. Share a huge ice cream sundae with one spoon.

140. Assign a "personal flower" to each other.

141. Drop raspberries in your champagne.

142. Wake up at dawn.

143. Stay up all night.

144. Watch a meteor shower.

145. Travel to where you can see the Northern Lights.

146. Shop for crystal.

147. Register as a bride (even if you've been married for years)!

148. Throw a huge party.

149. Have an intimate dinner party for two.

150. Have a water balloon fight.

151. Buy each other toe rings.

152. Ride a carousel. Try for the brass ring.

153. Feed each other cotton candy.

154. Feed peanuts to an elephant.

155. Have golf cart races.

156. Go to a drumming circle.

157. Sing songs out loud.

158. Have a barbecue.

159. Watch *The Princess Bride* together.

160. Watch *The Wedding Planner* together.

161. Watch *Palm Beach Story* together.

162. Give a gift for no reason.

163. Swim with the dolphins together.

164. Have a picnic in a busy park and people-watch.

165. Blow bubbles.

166. Take a boat trip to Martha's Vineyard.

167. Take a hot-air balloon ride.

168. Have picnic in the middle of a weekday.

169. Rent a glider plane.

170. Stay in a bed-and-breakfast.

171. Visit Niagara Falls.

172. Make a big salad together.

173. Go to a candy store and go wild!

174. Go to a concert and jump up and down like a teeny bopper.

175. Share a milkshake.

176. Share a perfect martini.

177. Take a cruise.

178. Go to a baseball game.

179. Eat hot dogs. Write each other's name with mustard.

180. Shell peanuts for each other.

181. Ride a Ferris wheel.

182. Kiss your lover's eyelashes.

183. Give your lover a ring from a gumball machine.

184. Walk along a wind-swept cliff.

185. Read your lover's palm.

186. Play in a Penny Arcade. Don't miss the photo booth.

187. Drink tea and read your lover's tea leaves.

188. Listen to a different kind of music.

189. Take a boat trip from Wales to Dublin.

190. Go see a psychic together.

191. Name a star or constellation after your lover.

192. Have a date in a bookstore.

193. Write a novel about your love.

194. Learn how to make your lover's favorite dish.

195. Play footsies.

196. Stroll up and down the avenue.

197. Count the hairs on his head.

198. Take a shower together.

199. Learn witchcraft together.

200. Knead bread or pizza crust together.

201. Make a romantic wish for the day.

202. Get matching tattoos.

203. Rent a limousine.

204. Wear a mask.

205. Tell your lover a romantic bedtime story.

206. Drink a toast to each other.

207. Buy each other new pajamas.

208. Leave a romantic message on your lover's voicemail or email.

209. Have a piece of romantic jewelry made for your lover.

210. Leave a rose on the bed.

211. Work out together.

212. Take a cooking class together.

213. Make music together.

214. Redecorate your house together.

215. Make French bread together.

216. Watch *My Fair Lady* together.

217. Watch *When Harry Met Sally* together.

218. Watch *Gentlemen Prefer Blondes* together.

219. Watch *The Bachelor* together.

220. Collect seashells.

221. Play air guitar together.

222. Go to Disney World or any amusement park together.

223. Wear nothing at all.

224. Ride a roller coaster together.

225. Ride an elephant together.

226. Learn to speak Italian together.

227. Sing an opera together.

228. Read *Romeo and Juliet* aloud.

229. Read any work by William Shakespeare together.

230. Watch the sunrise together

231. Watch the sunset together.

232. Go dancing in the rain.

233. Walk under an umbrella together.

234. Go out and pretend that you are on your first date.

235. Have a "tickle contest."

236. Sing Frank Sinatra songs together.

237. Buy lottery tickets together.

238. Feed each other raw oysters with extra horseradish.

239. Learn Yiddish together.

240. Spend the day pretending that you are your grandparents.

241. Buy Girl Scout cookies together.

242. Feed each other bologna sandwiches.

243. Dedicate a song to your lover on the radio.

244. Invent something.

245. Have chocolate strawberries delivered to your lover's workplace.

246. Buy your lover a new outfit.

247. Leave a Hershey's kiss under the pillow every night for a week.

248. See how long you can kiss without coming up for air.

249. Sneak into your lover's office and leave a Hershey's kiss in the desk or on the computer.

250. Build a scarecrow and put it up in your front lawn.

251. Invite your friends for cocktails.

252. Have a single rose delivered to your lover's gym.

253. Make out while a real estate person shows you a new place to live.

254. Go on a kid's pony ride.

255. Feed the seagulls.

256. Make your lover a surprise computer screen that opens up with a picture of the two of you.

257. Have sushi for breakfast, lunch, and dinner.

258. Shop for antiques.

259. Wear fake fur.

260. Send your lover a digital card.

261. Make a newsletter of the happy, romantic events in your lives and email it to your friends and family.

262. Read about a famous romance in history that you most admire.

263. Blow in your lover's ear.

264. Leave a bag of Lifesavers in your lover's pocket and write a note that says, "Our love has saved my life."
265. Join a peace protest.
266. Have a pillow fight.
267. Spend a night in the Honeymoon Suite of a tacky motel.
268. Assign a "personal day of the week" to each other (e.g. "Thursday is Jeff Day).
269. End every sentence you say to your lover with "I love you" for one whole day.
270. Stick a cherry in your lover's navel and pick it out with your teeth.
271. Make a happy face out of two sunny-side-up eggs and a strip of bacon and serve your lover breakfast in bed.
272. Leave your lover a surprise gift in a Cracker Jack box.
273. Put your lover's phone number in first place on speed dial.
274. Make something by hand, together.
275. Give your lover the paper ring off an expensive cigar.
276. Explore the attic.
277. Walk in the woods.
278. Write your lover's name on his hand in Pixie Stick candy and lick it off.
279. Twist your arms together and feed each other ice cream.
280. Shop for new colognes together.
281. Share a bowl of pasta. Eat each string starting at opposite ends until your lips meet.
282. Make out in the back seat of a bus.
283. Give your lover a bubble bath and scrub every inch of him.
284. Hold hands in church or temple.
285. Buy pizza for your lover's whole office staff.
286. Leave a Hershey's kiss by the toothpaste.
287. Kiss while waiting for the airplane to take off.

288. Trim each other's hair.

289. Go jogging together.

290. Make out in a lawyer's waiting room.

291. Take a trip on the Orient Express or any other train vacation.

292. Rent a sexy video.

293. Ask your lover to carry you across the threshold of your front door every day for a week.

294. Have a baby powder fight.

295. Speak to each other in an English accent all day for one day.

296. Take a karate class together.

297. Have an awards ceremony for anything great that your lover has just done.

298. Ice skate together.

299. Go cross-country skiing together.

300. Get full body massages.

301. Do a puzzle together.

302. Have go-cart races.

303. Take a long walk.

304. Get matching personalized license plates.

305. Have a basket of hot muffins delivered to your lover's workplace.

306. Shoot a whole roll of film just of each other's faces.

307. Watch *Love Story* together.

308. Watch *The Wizard of Oz* together.

309. Watch *Casablanca* together.

310. Watch *It's A Wonderful Life* together.

311. Leave a rose in the bathroom.

312. Roll down a hill and race each other back to the top.

313. Look for a lost item together.

314. Surprise each other with tickets to somewhere you've always wanted to go.

315. Play Jeopardy together.

316. Slow dance.

317. Go on a talk show together.

318. Eat at a buffet.

319. Give each other facials.

320. Get tickets to *Saturday Night Live*.

321. Tell each other secrets.

322. Have dinner or lunch under a bridge.

323. See how far you can walk while giving each other piggyback rides.

324. Read the story of Cleopatra, Julius Caesar, and Marc Antony. Plan to visit Egypt and sail down the Nile.

325. Feed the pigeons.

326. Go on a mission.

327. Give your lover a candy ring.

328. Visit the Vatican or any one of Italy's romantic sites.

329. Ride in a gondola.

330. Go out for a treat.

331. Smile all day.

332. Go on a fitness program or start a "get healthy" routine.

333. Bet on who's going to win on the latest reality show.

334. Tickle your lover's arm with your fingertips.

335. Make a list of all your exes and burn them in a ceremonial bonfire.

336. Climb a mountain together.

337. Wear bright colors.

338. Drive through the desert at night and count the stars.

339. Check into a spa for the weekend.

340. Embroider towels with both your initials.

341. Take turns being each other's "slave for a day."

342. Take a hot tub.

343. Send your lover a digital bouquet of flowers.

344. Drink Piña Coladas or Mai Tais under a palm tree together.

345. Groom a dog or cat.
346. Watch reruns of your favorite old TV shows together on Nick at Nite.
347. Paint your house (or a room) together.
348. Assign a "personal color" to each other.
349. Name your lover's underwear, socks, and shoes.
350. Shop for mattresses.
351. Visit a sex shop. Giggle.
352. Get hypnotized together.
353. Go on a treasure hunt together.
354. Go to the opera.
355. Email a picture of the two of you to all your friends and family.
356. Cuddle in the front seat.
357. Learn a magic trick together.
358. Knit scarves for each other.
359. Have breakfast by candlelight.
360. Have a picnic on the living room floor.
361. Experiment with proper technique for eating Oreos.
362. Go to a karaoke bar and let loose.
363. Go to a local high school musical.
364. Feed a llama.
365. Kiss under the mistletoe.

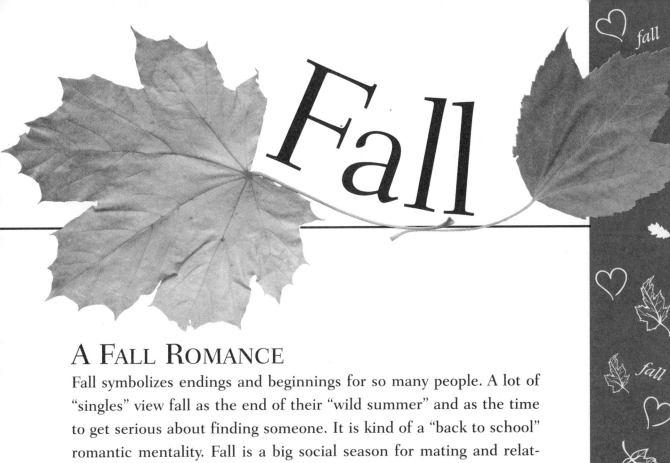

Fall

A FALL ROMANCE

Fall symbolizes endings and beginnings for so many people. A lot of "singles" view fall as the end of their "wild summer" and as the time to get serious about finding someone. It is kind of a "back to school" romantic mentality. Fall is a big social season for mating and relating—there are a multitude of ongoing events and activities.

As you move onto fall romance, remember that every day—rain or shine—is an opportunity to shower your lover with love and affection. No matter what the weather is outside, it is never too hot or too cold to have some romantic fun. Just because it's time to pack up the beach blankets and put away your bikini doesn't mean your love life has to cool down. (Hey, shorter days mean longer nights!!!) So when you start to feel that nip in the air, get ready for some serious snuggling as the leaves turn their beautiful fall colors.

MONDAY—FRIDAY AROMATHERAPY

Sunday

Relaxation: Patchouli

Patchouli oil can help you get a good night's rest. It can also be an aphrodisiac, in a warm and fuzzy, comfortable way.

Monday

Clarity: Rosemary

Rosemary is an herb that helps you operate on full throttle. It can assist in giving you the strength and clarity to make changes.

Tuesday

Balance: Rosewood

Rosewood can keep mature lovers in the mood for romance. For younger lovers, rosewood can help restore you to a soothing place of peace, balance, and harmony.

Wednesday

Healing: Lemon

Lemon inspires lovers to keep a positive attitude. A hot lemon oil massage is great for romantic healing.

Thursday

Rejuvenation: Mandarin

Mandarin helps soften the rough edges of your day and returns you to a gentle, carefree state of being. It will lighten your hearts and relieve your frustrations.

Friday

Passion: Palmarosa

Palmarosa will help you let go of the worries of the day and concentrate on your romantic relationship.

Saturday

Play: Pine

Rubbing pine oil on the soles of your feet and between your toes will uplift you and give you boundless energy.

FALL ACTIVITIES

Check In and Check Out
Make a date to call each other on the phone at least once a week just for a little "romantic pep talk." Tell each other what you love about one other and say, "You are the sunshine of my life."

Tan Man
Have a tanning date. Sometimes if you keep your summer glow a little longer than nature ordinarily would allow, you feel a nice little lift. Meet each other for a tanning session at a local salon, and bake away. For those of you who dread the thought of skin cancer or don't like to be enclosed in those claustrophobic beds, a good self-tanner will do the trick. You and your lover can have a blast covering each other's bodies in the stuff that makes you feel like "Malibu Barbie and Ken" all year long. Just make sure to wash your hands thoroughly afterwards unless you want to wake up with orange palms.

You Light Up My Life!
If you or your lover find yourselves lagging from lack of sunlight, go to a local hardware store or Home Depot and pick up full spectrum light bulbs, specially designed for people who suffer from Seasonal Affective Disorder (S.A.D.). With these special lights set up in a convenient area in your home, you and your lover will never have to sulk from lack of sunshine. Make it a point to hang out together in your "sunny spot."

Floridays
When all else fails, book a romantic weekend getaway to Miami, the Bahamas, Mexico, or San Juan. A fall getaway is just the ticket to perk up your romance!

Leaf Your Worries Behind

What fall lacks in heat it more than makes up for in color. Relish the crisp, cool air and fall back in love with this very romantic season with a little leaf-looking.

1. Rake your fallen leaves into a big pile, then run and jump right in with abandon. Don't be afraid to roll around like little kids and remember that excited feeling.

2. Take a drive through the countryside where you can see all the leaves turning gorgeous fall reds, browns, oranges, and yellows. When the sun is shining you'll be dazzled by Mother Nature's brilliant fall exhibition of colors. This is a great way to welcome in the fall season.

Nectar of the Gods

Fall is the harvest season for some of the world's most exquisite wines. You and your lover can enjoy the nectar from the fruit of the vine by checking out a vineyard near you. A lot of vineyards will offer extensive wine courses and lectures during the harvest season. Of course, you can probably find some brilliant wine tastings and full course gourmet dinners. Enjoy sampling the different vintages while you savor sumptuous treats. If there is no vineyard by you then check with your local restaurants, gourmet clubs, liquor stores, or anywhere in your area you can buy fine wine. Many of these places offer promotional complementary wine tastings during the harvest season.

A Private Tasting

Of course you can always have your own wine tasting at home with a group of friends, or privately with just your lover. Buy a selection of wines that you've never heard of and some crackers and exotic cheese.

The next thing you know you and your lover have transformed your house into a "Oenophile's delight."

Wine Weekend

For lovers who are more serious winers and diners, you can book a trip to California's Napa Valley or Bordeaux, France, for a gourmet tour of the vineyards. A lot of wineries worldwide offer extensive hospitality tours that can include nights spent in châteaux (castles) and "grape picker" farmhouse lunches. To decide what area of the world to visit, just look on the label and see where your favorite wine originates. If you are an American Express Platinum Card Carrying Member, then their twenty-four-hour travel concierge can make arrangements for you. If not, a local travel agent should have plenty of wine weekend information.

On the Auction Block

Call Christie's, Phillips, Butterfield's, or Sotheby's in New York and inquire about their international wine auctions. You and your lover might get a kick out of watching wine being sold at $1000 a bottle and up. (They do have some lower priced ones, too.) Who knows? You may want to treat yourselves to a romantic, frivolous splurge and buy a bottle of 1967 Chateux D'Yquem or a magnum of Crystal.

Gorgeous Grapes

You don't have to be a world-class connoisseur to allow the love of wine to enhance your romance. Here is a romantic guide to wine that will make it more accessible. Following are the types of grapes for which wines are named, with some secret hints about how these naughty little fruits can act as powerful aphrodisiacs. Now, when a waiter asks, "Would you like a Merlot or a Pinot Noir?" you can order the wine that best fits your current romantic mood!

BARBERA

An earthy, robust grape that can bring out the Barbarian in you. Drink it slowly, and even the most timid will discover the wild thing within!

CABERNET FRANC

Creating a taste that is both sweet and herbaceous, these soft grapes will put the spring back into your step, and make you get all "kissy face" with the one you love.

CABERNET SAUVIGNON

If you are involved in a royal romance, these are the crème de la crème of rich, regal grapes. After a glass you will feel powerful and in control.

CHARDONNAY

These potent grapes produce a rich, almost creamy taste combined with a fruity simplicity that will make you feel like snuggling and cuddling.

CHENIN BLANC

These grapes will put you in a carefree, laid back, "anything goes" mood. For some easy, smooth drinking, Chenin Blanc is perfect for an afternoon barbecue or dining "al fresco."

GAMAY

The young, fruity, and whimsical taste of these grapes are known to make even the most mature lovers feel like kids again. This is a great wine when you and your lover need an evening of light-hearted love and affection.

GARNACHA

A seduction secret of the Spanish for many centuries, these grapes have the flair of Latin love and Flamenco flaming passion. They can add a little mystery to any romance from Madrid to Minneapolis.

MELON
Because of it's dry, direct taste, you and your lover may find yourselves reading *War and Peace* together, or having a cerebral conversation about the origin of life.

MERLOT
These rotund, chubby little grapes will make you feel warm and fuzzy inside. Grab your lover like a much loved teddy bear and show him how to heat up a nippy fall evening.

MULLER-THURGAU
If you are a simple, no-frills "minimalist" at heart, then you will enjoy a glass of wine made with these grapes. This is for lovers who take themselves very seriously!

NEBBIOLO
Think pizza and lasagna—these Italian home-grown goodies will make you and your lover become absolutely "Moonstruck." That's amoré!

PETITE SYRAH
These left coast crazies will have you and your lover California dreamin' in no time. They produce rich, deep glasses of intense, romantic wine.

PINOT BLANC
These grapes are a favorite in France for making fun, fruity, and often flirty glasses of the white stuff. They are great for a casual come-on or a lover's languid liaison.

PINOT NOIR
Grown in cool, crisp climates, these grapes produce soft, subtle wine that can make a fall evening feel like summer all over again.

RIESLING
You and your lover will adore the fruity, fragrant bouquet of Riesling grapes. A bottle of this wine will make you feel like you are standing in a field of your favorite flowers.

SANGIOVESE
A down-home, hearty type of grape that makes a meaty glass of wine. Watch out, it is known to bring out the lusty peasant in the most proper princess!

SAUVIGNON BLANC
For lovers who are in the mood for a stress-free day outdoors, these grapes make the wine for sporty types. Great with food, sauvignon blanc is perfect for a picnic in the park when you decide to give your "relationship" a rest!

SEMILLON
When you're ready for romance, these grapes create a glass of wine that tells your lover you are so ripe they need to taste you before you fall from the tree.

SHIRAZ
If underneath your business suit you are a saucy little tart at heart, then these are the grapes for the shameless hussy in you.

SYLVANDER
Don't have a big budget for a night of wining and dining? Have no

fear, Sylvander grapes make a wine that will give you and your lover a night of affordable affection.

SYRAH
Unlike the Petite Syrah, this rambunctious, robust bunch of black grapes makes a glass of wine that demands your full respect and attention.

TEMPRILLO
Like a temptress from the land of macho Matadors and raging bulls, these grapes have Spanish eyes that can work as a sexy aphrodisiac.

ZINFANDEL
This native son "good ol' boy" grape makes a wine that is unique to American soil. When you and your lover want to feel passionately patriotic, a bottle of Zinfandel at your Thanksgiving meal will make you swoon.

Apple-picking
For a simple, yet delightful, fall treat, go apple-picking at a local orchard. Afterwards, you and your lover can make some heartwarming fall dishes starring your pick of the day, like Apple Cobbler, Apple Brown Betty, Cinnamon Spiced Applesauce, Coconut and Raisin Baked Apples, and, of course, good old fashioned Deep Dish Apple Pie. These treats should fill you up and put smiles on your faces.

Take a Hay Ride
This is a wonderful way to enjoy an old fashioned romance. Call around to your local farmers or produce stands and find out if anyone is offering a fall hay ride. You'll have a wonderful time keeping each other warm in the crisp fall night air, with the stars above, and the smell of wood smoke in the air.

Get a Fall Makeover

Every year the cosmetic companies come out with their latest renditions of deep, rich fall colors. Just for some romantic fun, first arrange to meet your lover for dinner at a romantic restaurant known for its atmosphere. Then, go to a makeup counter at your local department store and have the beautician give you a dramatic fall makeover. If you are not normally a gal who wears a lot of makeup, this will be a unique treat (who knows, your lover may not even recognize you). This type of makeover will give you a sophisticated, dark aura that can be very titillating to a lover who is used to seeing you with a naked face (or with just a hint of lipstick.) If you are the type of gal who doesn't leave the house without a show-stopping display of makeup every morning, then take time to really develop your mysterious fall "look." Your lover will enjoy seeing you looking so dramatic just for him! He'll appreciate you taking the time to really take care of yourself.

Get a Life

If you or your lover are thinking about making a career move or change of any kind, fall is the perfect time to do so. People are back from summer vacations, and there is generally a "let's get back to work" attitude in most companies, with renewed motivation running high. If you are thinking of starting your own business, fall is a great time for that, too. Acting as a support system for one another while you both pursue your career dreams is an essential part of any romantic relationship. When you can use each other as a sounding board to bounce your plans off, the two of you have a better chance of reaching your goals. Remember that a little love goes a long way in helping someone be the best he or she can be.

ROMANTIC FALL GETAWAYS

Fall is a wonderful time to plan a romantic escape with the one you love. This is also a great romantic season to be outside because the weather is neither too hot nor too cold. Make sure to select a destination where you and your lover can take advantage of this inviting outdoor season.

1. Tuscany, Italy

Located in the north of Italy, not too far from the Swiss border, the mountains of Tuscany have some of the most lovely and lush landscapes you will ever see. And if that were not enough, the sweet, pungent aroma of olives and grapes growing all over the countryside will seduce you to no end. A week in Tuscany does wonders to regenerate the heart and soul. Treat yourselves to a local Italian wine and cheese harvest-time festival, or spoil yourselves rotten at the world famous Montecatini Spa. People come from all over the world to drink the "waters" of Montecatini—it is Italy's answer to the fountain of youth.

2. The Berkshire Mountains, Massachusetts

After the summer crowds of the internationally acclaimed Tanglewood Music Festival have all gone home, the Berkshires return to quiet serenity. Perfect for anyone who could use some fresh mountain air, the Berkshires provide an easily accessible retreat from the hustle and bustle of the "real world." Check out a romantic Colonial bed-and-breakfast, or pitch a tent in one of the many parks and campgrounds. No matter how you choose to do it in the Berkshires, you and your lover can enjoy a sexy, secluded time away.

3. The Loire Valley, France

If you need to get the *joie de vivre* back into your relationship, then take a trip to the irresistibly romantic Loire Valley this fall. Its winding rivers and rolling hills, as well as harvest-time wine tastings, can get anyone in the mood for love! Enjoy dining on some local gourmet favorites, such as *fois gras*, cassoulet, and a rich red wine.

4. Santa Barbara, California

Just an hour-and-a-half north of Los Angeles lies an unspoiled paradise called Santa Barbara. With sweeping views overlooking the Pacific Ocean and fresh salt air, this low-key town is a haven for those who want to escape the smog and fog of Hollywood. Celebrities and civilians alike have found a stress-free oasis in the Santa Ynez, Montecito, and Camerillo areas of Santa Barbara. You can ride on horseback through the hills, catch a polo game, take a walk along the beach, or enjoy one of the best margaritas you'll ever have on Main Street. Slip on your sandals and baggy beach pants to enjoy a cool getaway in this special place, just a stone's throw off California's famous Pacific Coast Highway.

5. Ireland

Ireland is a gorgeous place to visit any time of the year, but most especially in the fall. Enjoy the rock and roll nightlife scene of Dublin's Temple Bar area. Savor a few pints of Guinness, and visit the places where the Irish band U2 got its start. Spend weekends exploring Celtic castles or fairy tale, cobblestoned, windswept towns along the coast. The countryside of Ireland is a perfect mix of the ancient and modern romance. You and your lover may just find yourselves leaving the land of Eire with a four-leaf clover of love!

6. Wales

The author of this book is very partial to the tiny country of Wales, because that is where she found her prince (actually he was born in Wales and living in London)! However, most people don't think of Wales as a romantic vacation spot and they are sorely missing out on this tiny seaside treasure. The waves crashing along the cliffs of Ogmor and Porth Cawl are a breathtaking romantic sight that you will never forget. Just twenty minutes away in the Welsh capital of Cardiff, there are gorgeous new hotels, shops, and restaurants surrounding ancient castles. The fall is a particularly lovely time in Wales because the weather is still warm enough to stroll by the sea. Take a trip to Wales, and the next time you kiss your lover, he may just turn into a prince!

7. Germany

Germany is a terrific country to visit during the fall, especially during late September to early October. This is the time of Octoberfest, Germany's national beer-guzzling, polka-dancing, sausage-eating holiday! The streets of Munich turn into one big, happy party during this time of year. Everybody, young and old, is in the mood for love and laughter. Do the "chicken dance," get yourselves some sauerbraten and a big mug of brew while you join in the fun! After a week of all that good eating and drinking, check into Brenner's spa at Baden-Baden for some healthy, romantic "R&R," or head up to Bavaria for a hike in the mountains. When all is said and done, Germany can provide you and your lover with a raucous and romantic fall retreat.

8. Indiana

This fall, put the heart back in your relationship by visiting America's heartland. Take a drive through the plains of Indiana and enjoy an all-American romance. Enjoy a down-home meal of chicken and biscuits, sit on the porch of a big old farmhouse and count the stars in the sky. You don't have to travel to a far-away country to enjoy an exotic romantic getaway. To "city folk," a weekend like this is a romantic world away from their demanding urban existence.

9. Connecticut

It's a shame poor Connecticut doesn't get as much holiday hype as the rest of the surrounding New England states, because it is actually an incredibly beautiful and romantic place to visit. Situated on the shores of the Long Island Sound, there are several historic sights to explore and romantic country inns to stay in nestled in quaint little towns. Old Greenwich is a particularly exquisite exclusive hamlet that is home to mind-boggling mansions and endless green pastures. If you and your lover find the home of your dreams in Old Greenwich, but don't have the cash to buy the door knob…that's no problem. Connecticut is home to two huge casino resorts (Foxwoods and Mohegan Sun), both of which are on Indian reservations. You can make a mint, then sail away out of Old Mystic seaport. Connecticut creates the perfect atmosphere for warm, cozy love and intimacy this fall.

10. Oklahoma

Are you and your lover ready for a whole lot of love with a real Western flair? How about moseying on down to the Cowboy Hall of Fame in Oklahoma City for a romantic covered wagon trip back in time? Down in Tulsa, home of the American Quarter Horse Association, you and your lover can watch one of the finest equestrian competitions in the U.S. These ponies will amaze you with their versatility, strength, and style. A day at "The World" will make you and your lover want to ride off into the blazing Oklahoma sunset, never to be seen again!

September

Labor Day (First Monday in September)

This holiday is the official end of summer. View it as a beginning for welcoming in another romantic season. There are a lot of things the two of you can do to enjoy a romantic Labor Day—here are some suggestions.

1. A Labor of Love

If you and your lover have a beach house or rented somewhere for the summer, Labor Day weekend most often will be your last weekend together there. To make the "end of summer house cleanup" go swiftly and painlessly, put on some fun music while you sweep, pack, and scrub, and take lots of breaks to smile at and kiss each other. If you and your lover had an especially romantic time there, write a lovely letter to your landlord telling him what special memories the place will always hold for you both (just be sure that you get your first month's deposit back first).

2. Gotta Love that Barbecue

Like any other mild weather holiday, Americans can't wait to fire up the grill, stick some beer in a cooler and have a good ol' barbecue. Make this one extra romantic by grilling some exotic foods (other than hot dogs and hamburgers) like partridge, buffalo, alligator, tofu, or seitan (for the vegetarians). Just because it's an all-American holiday doesn't mean you can't experiment with some creative cuisine.

3. Re-Commit to Commitment

Labor Day is a great time for a romantic "re-commitment ceremony." You and your lover can have a big party and invite all your friends to witness this lovely occasion or just privately sneak off to a romantic location (like the end of a pier, a mountain top or a lakeside beach). No matter how you choose to do it, expressing to each other your feelings of love is always a very special way to end the summer.

The Autumnal Equinox (September 21st)

The autumnal equinox is the official start of autumn. On this day, daylight and dark are of equal lengths, but the days will start to get shorter and the nights longer. You'll want to grab all the sunlight you can from now until spring. Today, or sometime this week (weather permitting), grab lunch outside at the park, sitting on a city bench or out in your backyard. Enjoy the pleasure of each other's company while soaking up what's left of the sun's rays.

The Jewish High Holidays: Rosh Hashannah and Yom Kippur, A Time for Celebration and Contemplation (Varies each year, but is usually in September)

These two holidays that annually take place in mid- to late-September have a deep meaning for Jewish people around the world. Rosh Hashannah is the beginning of the New Year according to the Hebrew calendar. It is believed that on this day God decides who will be inscribed in the "Book of Life" for another year, and on Yom Kipper the Book is sealed. This is a festive holiday featuring apples and honey to start the year off on a sweet note. Yom Kippur is considered the holiest day of the Jewish year, because it is the Day of Atonement. This is a day to recognize your sins, make peace with those you've hurt and also with God, and to be forgiven so you can begin the year with a clean slate.

&❧ **On Rosh Hashannah, write your lover a list of all the "sweet" things he has done for you during the year.**

꙰ On Yom Kippur, apologize for anything you've done that has hurt or angered your lover, and be prepared to forgive all that has hurt you. Don't dwell on ways that you have hurt each other. "I love you, I'm sorry," will do.

꙰ Go down to a river or stream (it should be moving water) with some hunks of torn up bread. Throw them in the water to symbolize your wrongdoings being washed away.

꙰ Do one really great thing for each other to make up for all the "not so nice" things you might have done during the year.

꙰ Finish the day with a festive meal and dancing. This symbolizes renewal of your relationship and starting off again with a "clean slate."

꙰ If you are Jewish, please GO TO TEMPLE (even if this is the only time of year that you go). You and your lover will get a renewed sense of faith and an added dimension of spirituality to your relationship. Besides, your mother will be so happy!

ROMANTIC SIGN

VIRGO (August 24th – Sept 22nd)

Symbol: A young girl in a boat with an ear of corn and a torch in her hand.

Ruling Planet: Mercury

Rules: Intestines, Hip area

Gem Stone: Rock Crystal Egg

Good Characteristics: high standards, focused, good worker, analytical, wants to improve things, detailed, methodical, studious.

Bad Characteristics: too critical, can freak out when something isn't perfect, lonely, not a good self-promoter, can get frustrated or depressed very easily.

Romantic Catch Phrase: "This relationship is near perfection!"

What It Means: "You almost meet my incredibly high standards."

What It Really Means: "Thanks for sticking with me even though I am such a picky control freak."

Most Romantic Thing You Can Say to a Virgo: "You've made my life perfectly romantic."

Top Ten Gifts for a Virgo:

1. A "How-To" book on anything.
2. Send a cleaning crew or a maid to clean your lover's house from top to bottom.
3. The video *Analyze This* with Billy Crystal and Robert DeNiro.
4. Hire a company to organize the closet.
5. Have all his/her shoes polished.
6. Have all his/her suits cleaned and pressed.
7. A custom made suit or gown.
8. If you live together, arrange all YOUR stuff, the way they do theirs.
9. An exotic wine, foreign language, or financial investing course.
10. A hand-made parchment scroll that lists "Ten Reasons Why I Think You're Perfect."

African Astrology Symbol:

The Voyager (September 4th – October 3rd)

Body Type: Sturdy and strong.

Personality Traits: Adventurous, ultra-sensitive, role model, hopeful, optimistic, encouraging, no sense of limiting boundaries.

Most Romantic Gift: Flying lessons

Favorite Colors: Bright, sunny yellows

How To Win Their Heart Forever: Keep moving and encourage them to explore new places. Partake in their "life's an adventure" attitude!

October

Halloween (October 31st)

This kooky, spooky fall holiday is the perfect time to get romantically bewitched. Even though to most of us, Halloween means little more than dressing-up in costumes and "trick-or-treating," this is the perfect holiday to explore the mystical side of romantic rituals and visions.

1. The Romantic Trick-or-Treat

If you and your lover liked Trick-or-Treating as children and want to try an adult version of this Halloween tradition, then do the following. Fill up two "his" and "hers" bags with candy and naughty treats. Examples of "naughty" treats are edible underwear, edible and scented body lubricant, adult magazines, and movies. Before opening your "goody" bags, dress up in Halloween costumes. You can create these yourselves by going to the lingerie store or looking in the Frederick's of Hollywood catalogue. After both you are all dressed up, take turns opening each other's goodie bags. Now play!

2. Hocus Pocus, Get Your Romantic Relationship Into Focus!

Given the fact that you are a rational human being, you probably don't believe in the power of magic spells and witchcraft. However, if you have an open mind and, more importantly, an open heart, you can tap into the Universal Law and Power of Attraction to fortify your relationship. You just have to focus your energy and use these magical rituals that have enhanced romance through the ages. (Remember, it's not the symbols in the rituals that help you achieve your desired romantic result, the power of attraction ALWAYS starts with you!)

- Go to the park and write your lover's name in pebbles or branches.

- Throw a penny or a pebble into a brook and make three romantic wishes or declarations of love.

- Roll around in a pile of leaves three times, shouting your lover's name backwards.

- Make marshmallow and raisin figures of you and your lover, then roast them together on a stick.

- Carve both of your names and birthdays into a big red candle. Let it burn out.

- Make a "spellbinding" love potion. Mix cranberry juice, pineapple juice, coconut milk, and orange juice, and serve with a strawberry or lime garnish. For more powerful magic, you can always add a little vodka!

- Make up a secret magic word. Every time one of you says your magic word, you have to kiss each other passionately.

- Why not have fun hypnotizing your lover? The power of suggestion is an extremely effective tool in the area of love and romance. Ask your lover to lie down on a couch and get comfortable. Then tell him to count backwards from one hundred. When he gets to the number one, he should be totally relaxed. Give him romantic suggestions like "On the count of three, you find me absolutely irresistible and can't stop kissing me." Count to three, snap your fingers and see what happens!

A LITTLE WHITE MAGIC

In many cultures, from ancient pagan times, through Greek and Roman mythology, all the way to today's technologically advanced societies, people have used props and rituals to focus their personal powers and create magic. Why not have some fun employing ancient techniques to create a little white magic in your romance? You don't necessarily have to invoke the power of the gods to cast a romantic spell or attract someone to you. Following are adaptations of some fascinating classic love rituals for you to explore.

Latin Love Rituals: Meet Me in Miami for Mucho Magic!

The mystical practices of Santeria originated with the Yoruba Tribe in Nigeria, Africa, then found their way to Cuba and South America. Just as Greek and Roman mythology honor Venus or Juno as the goddess of love, in Santeria, the spectacular goddess "Oshun" dominates the world of love and romance. Oshun symbolizes the qualities traditionally associated with female energy, such as nurturing, care-giving, loving, romance, inner strength, fertility, and softness. Here are a few "beginner" ideas to focus your mind on improving your romance.

PUMPKIN POWER

If you want to enhance the wonderful nurturing qualities that are uniquely female in your life, tap into the universal energy source by offering a gift to Oshun. Traditionally a pumpkin is considered the appropriate gift, which makes the perfect symbol to invoke your Halloween love! Set up a display of cheerful yellow pumpkins and be reminded of the power of female energy.

LOVE BEADS

In Santeria, it is customary to wear a beaded necklace to symbolize the connection between humankind and the gods. The necklace that is symbolic of Oshun's female powers consists of ten yellow beads followed by five red ones. Wear these beads to symbolize that you are on a mission of love! From a truly romantic standpoint, every time you pass a mirror and see yourself with the necklace on, or any time you feel it around your neck, you will be reminded to do something special for your lover. Even if it means just calling to say "I love you" or leaving a sweet note in his briefcase, when you are wearing an "Oshun" necklace, you can't help but remember to add romance into your life.

OSHUN'S MAGIC SPELLS

1. "Bathing Beauty" Spell

Call on your lover's sense of smell when you want to induce strong emotions. It's as easy as bathing in aphrodisiac perfumes. Fill your bathtub with water and add cinnamon and rose oil. Float some gardenia flowers on top if possible; or get yourself gardenia-scented bubble bath. The combination of these enticing scents should put your lover in the mood for romance as soon as they get close to you.

2. "I'm in You" Spell

This is an ancient spell found in many magical traditions. It is believed that your lover will find you completely irresistible if he subconsciously tastes some of you in the meal!. With an eyedropper, snap up a few drops of salt water, meant to represent your tears. Simply take the "tear-filled" eyedropper and season the salad dressing or another dish with the salt of your tears. If the ancient legends prove to be true, your lover won't be able to tear himself away from you.

3. "Honey, I'm Stuck on You" Spell

Retrieve a lock of your lover's hair from his hairbrush. Then take a lock of your own hair and place the locks together on a square of plain brown paper. Drip a couple of drops of honey on top, fold, and stick it together. Put the paper in a special hiding place. When you are alone, take out the paper and light a red candle. Hold the candle over the paper so that the red wax drips onto it. This ritual will help focus your mind on the importance of "sticking together" through thick and thin.

4. "Stand by Your Man" Spell

If you and your lover are having a lovers' quarrel or going through an unpleasant time, it's important to bring the focus back to what is good and basic about the relationship. Get a small, white piece of paper and a red ink pen and write your names in a spiral around each other, seven times. Pick a special place to keep the paper, or bury it outside when the moon is full. Think of some of the things you like best about each other, and speak those things as you do the ritual. Using this little ritual can help you and your lover focus on re-dedicating yourselves to the relationship.

5. " Freeze the Threat" Ritual

Is someone outside your relationship posing a romantic threat? Let's say that you and your lover have a great relationship, but there is someone in his office who keeps flirting and asking him out. If this bothers you despite the lack of interest on the part of your lover, maybe you should gently "freeze" the threat out of your mind. Just write the person's name on a piece of paper in a circle seven times and then write your lover's name next to it in the same fashion. Wrap the paper up in a small piece of black cloth and tie it up with a red string. Stick it in a small container, pour some cold water over it, then stick it in the freezer and forget about it.

6. "Step on It" Spell

Did you know that there is an artery in your left foot that goes directly to your heart? Some believe that if you attach a message to the bottom of your foot and walk around on it all day, it sends a powerful message of love to the Universe. Take a piece of paper and write your name and your lover's name in a circle. Add some rose oil and cinnamon powder. Fold up the paper and seal it with tape. Use more tape to strap the note onto the bottom of your foot. You can leave it on all day and forget about it, or stomp on it purposely and energetically to send your love intention out to the universe!

The Witches' Candle Guide

Nothing helps quiet your mind like focusing on the flame of a burning candle. When you put all of your attention on the light, you shut out all other distractions. Candlelight also symbolizes healing and an eternal source of energy. Empower your romance by using a variety of candles to represent the positive elements of your relationship. By accentuating the goodness in your relationship and the positive personality qualities that you and your lover share, you are strengthening the relationship on all levels. Below is a list of candle colors that you can use for your own private rituals and ceremonies:

Red: love, sex, stamina, passion, fire.
Green: money, prosperity, fertility, good health, and wellness.
White: purity, spirituality, truth, justice.
Blue: commitment, spirituality, compassion, sweetness.
Silver: winning, overcoming obstacles, surviving bad times.
Yellow: good looks, appeal, attraction.
Orange: happiness, celebration, intellectual stimulation, mind expansion.

Purple: nobility, royalty, wealth, fame, worship, intuition.
Peach: neutrality, comfort, love, nurturing.
Grey: peace, serenity, balance, easy-going, relaxation.

Dress For Success

Celebrate the inner goddess and your mystical relationship with nature and the universe by putting on your most self-affirming outfit—the one that makes you feel wild and unrestricted and beautiful. Give the blow dryer a rest and let your hair be tousled and free. Know that you are perfectly beautiful just the way you are. The important part of performing any kind of ritual is a renewed sense of self-worth, personal empowerment, and connectedness. And who knows? With the help of a little magic, you might just conjure up the perfect romance!

THE WHEN, WHERE, AND HOW OF MAGIC

Of course, Halloween is the perfect night for a witch to do her work, but if you are too busy trick-or-treating, then any night will do! According to *The Magic of Candle Burning*, by Donna Rose (Mi-World Publishing, 1995), Friday is the best day to do a romantic spell because it coordinates with Venus, the "love" planet. Where you cast your spells is ultimately up to you, but if you can do them outside on a moonlit autumn night, so much the better. Being outside in the brisk evening air can give you a sense that nature is alive and ready to work with you! Listed below are some innovative love spells designed especially for the romantic.

Love in a Jar

What you need:
13 small red candles or one big one
A snippet from any article of your lover's clothing
A strand of their hair

A snippet from any article of your clothing

A strand of your hair

Rose oil and rose petals

Cinnamon powder

Honey

A bit of red string

A small jar that you don't mind losing. Make sure that the jar can be sealed

Directions:

Put on your favorite goddess outfit. Go outside at midnight and find a special place to work your magic. You can set up a small folding table in the backyard for this purpose. The top of a stone wall or a clearing in the woods is also good.

Put the snippets of cloth and hair in the jar. Sprinkle in the cinnamon, rose petals, honey, and red string. Surround the jar with the candles and light them.

As you are lighting the candles, focus your eyes on the flames. Make three "air circles" around them with your hands. Then cover your eyes with your hands. With your eyes still closed, envision a white light washing through your body and circling above your head. As you envision the white light glowing through your body, invoke the higher powers.

Envision you and your lover doing something incredibly romantic. Concentrate on how it feels to be so in love and romantically content. By giving energy to those good feelings you are reinforcing the likelihood that they will be a part of your life.

After completing your visualization, find a place to bury the jar where you can find and revisit it. Anytime that you need a romantic "lift," light a candle and go back to the spot where you buried the jar. Take a few minutes to recall your romantic visualization and recreate those feelings of abundant love.

The Magic Picture Board

This is a manifestation exercise to help you visualize the romantic future you would like to make real.

What you need:
Pictures, either taken with your camera or cut out of a magazine, of things that represent what you would like to have in your romantic future, such as: a picture of you and your lover, wedding clothes, your dream honeymoon destination, your future children, your dream home, your dream romantic vacation spot, or anything that's important to your lives together

A big piece of poster board

Glue

Colored glitter

Construction paper

Magic markers

An array of brightly colored candles (consult the Witches' Candle Guide above to help you choose colors that have special meaning for you)

Directions:
First, arrange the pictures on the poster board in collage fashion until they are the way you want them to look. As you glue them on the poster board, envision a circle of white light around each picture. Imagine how it would feel to be wearing the wedding dress, taking the dream honeymoon, or living in the dream house. Focus on the emotions behind enjoying true romantic fulfillment.

Write down inspirational romantic words on the colored paper with the magic markers. As you write the words, don't forget to feel their meaning. For example, if you write down the word "commitment," experience the feeling of having a totally committed relationship. If you write down "passion," then relive in your mind a passionate moment in your recent romantic history. The trick is to "re-experience" the meaning of the word as you glue it to the Magic Picture Board.

When you have finished gluing on the words and pictures, lightly sprinkle the whole thing with colored glitter to add sparkle to your dreams.

Mount your completed board in a place where you can focus on and enjoy it at any time. Line up the colored candles in front of it and light each one (far enough away that the board doesn't catch on fire!), adding the qualities they represent to the fulfillment of your romantic dreams and goals.

The Magical Halloween Feast

As simple as making a delicious home-cooked meal for your lover may sound, when done as a love ritual, it can have magical effects on your romance. The difference is the consciousness you bring to the occasion. You are not just cooking dinner, you're creating a "love offering." Find out what your lover's favorite foods are, and design a menu to satisfy his desires. Make sure you have at least a three-course meal and good wine or other special beverage. Unless one of you is allergic, it never hurts to include chocolate. Make a grocery list of all the ingredients you'll need to make the dishes on the menu. Even if you are not used to cooking, if you base your meal on high quality ingredients, and prepare it with love, you can't go wrong!

What you need:
Parchment paper or other lovely paper on which to write the menu
A calligrapher's pen
A gorgeous tablecloth
Your best silverware and glasses
Special wine goblets

Colored candles (consult the Witches' Candle Guide and procure the ones that symbolize the emotions you want to arouse)
A single rose to place across each dish

What to Do:
Set the table in your best romantic fashion. Write the menu carefully on the parchment paper in your best penmanship using the calligrapher's pen. Name the dishes lovingly after the emotions or actions you want to evoke.

Sample Menu

Appetizer
French Kiss Onion Soup, or Passionate Proscuitto
with Honey-I-Do Melon
Salad
Seize Me Caesar Salad or Heavenly Hearts of Palm
with Luscious Lover's Lettuce
Main Course
Seduce Me Salmon or Cherish Me Chicken
Dessert
Over the Moon Peach Melba or
Lover's Forever Hot Fudge Sundaes

While you are preparing the meal, make sure that you visualize the feeling or emotion that you want each dish to invoke; for example, envision yourselves cherishing each other as you prepare the chicken. Conjure up your purest white light with which to infuse the food.

Light the candles and serve the food with care and style. Before you eat, join hands, close your eyes, and say the blessing of your choice, or use this affirmation:

"This meal is an offering to celebrate our divine love.
May the energy from this delicious food nourish our bodies,
And ignite an eternal romantic union in our souls.
We ask the Universal Energy Source
To help us keep the power of passion alive
Forever and ever...if this is to our highest good.
Amen."

Pour the wine into special goblets and hold it in your hands. Twist your arms around each other so that they become intertwined. Pour little droplets of the wine into each other's mouths and end with a passionate kiss! Then savor your meal, watching the glow of candlelight reflecting in each other's eyes.

Create Your Own Spellbinding Love Oil

The most powerful magic is the kind you make up yourself! Create a special "love oil" dedicated to the one you love. Start with almond, sesame, or baby oil as a base. Add some of your favorite aromatherapy essential oils. Keep in mind the scents preferred by your lover as well. Using visualization, focus on your most romantic feelings while you make your aphrodisiac. Keep the image of your lover before you and contemplate all the things you love most about him. Put all this good energy into your potion. Then, before you and your lover share a night of passion, anoint yourself with a little dab of your special oil on your wrists, on the nape of your neck or anywhere else, and ignite some magic sparks between the two of you.

ROMANTIC SIGN

LIBRA (*September 23rd – October 23rd*)
Symbol: A Set of Scales
Ruling Planet: Venus
Rules: The Kidneys
Gem Stone: Chrysophrase
Good Characteristics: comforting, flexible, friendly, fashionable, balanced, positive outlook, good diplomat, very likable.
Bad Characteristics: critical, hypersensitive, says yes to everybody, waits too long to make a decision, says bad things behind other people's back, narcissistic.
Romantic Catch Phrase: "I think I love you."
What It Means: "I think I love you, but I need to keep my options open."
What It Really Means: "I really do love you, but I don't want anyone else to feel left out."
Most Romantic Thing You Can Say to a Libra: "You keep me balanced and make me happy. We are in perfect harmony."

Top Ten Gifts for a Libra:

1. A trip to a smorgasbord buffet.
2. A trip to the United Nations.
3. A yearly subscription to the *National Enquirer,* the *Globe,* and the *Star.*
4. Tickets to a Tony Robbins seminar.
5. *The Power of Positive Thinking* by Dale Carnegie.
6. A weekend getaway to a place you know he loves, but would never admit it.
7. A big piece of jewelry.
8. Tickets to a big celebrity benefit.

9. A whole day of pampering at a day spa.

10. A fun, flashy sports car.

AFRICAN ASTROLOGY SYMBOL:

The Long Road (October 4th – November 3rd)

Body Type: Limber and flexible, youthful glow and ruddy complexion.

Personality Traits: Spontaneous, exuberant, creative, spiritual, non-conformist, passionate.

Most Romantic Gift: A new boat or DVD player.

Favorite Colors: Golds

How To Win Their Heart Forever: Keep it fun and light.

November

Thanksgiving (last Thursday of November)

Thanksgiving is a day of festivities, food, fun, and family. Thanksgiving can be a very romantic time for you and your lover not only to enjoy a great meal, but also to acknowledge the things that you are grateful for in your relationship. Start by giving each other a list of everything that you are thankful for about each other. After your Thanksgiving meal is eaten, spend the rest of the evening cuddling on the couch or in front of the fire. Basking in the warm glow of each other's love is a lot to be thankful for this fall!

ROMANTIC SIGN

SCORPIO (October 24th – November 27th)

Symbol: Scorpion
Ruling Planet: Mars
Rules: The genitals
Gem Stone: Serpentine
Good Characteristics: capable of a deep level of feeling on a mental, physical, spiritual, and emotional basis, loves to help people who are down and out, ethical, loves to be stimulated, reasonable, deeply intuitive.
Bad Characteristics: fanatical, becomes a victim, gets intimate too quickly then pulls away, controlling, vengeful, has a "My way or the highway" attitude, can turn on you very easily.
Romantic Catch Phrase: "You excite my mind, body, and soul!"
What It Means: "You excite my mind, body, and soul, even if I just met you ten minutes ago."

What It Really Means: "I really want to be excited by you all the time."

Most Romantic Thing You Can Say to a Scorpio: "You make my body and soul burn with desire."

Top Ten Gifts for a Scorpio:

1. The *Kama Sutra*.
2. A subscription to *Oui* magazine.
3. A new collection of porno tapes.
4. Frank Sinatra's *Greatest Hits* (all volumes).
5. *The Art Of Seduction*.
6. *Tapping Into Your Own Psychic Ability* by Edgar Cayce.
7. *Forever* by Judy Bloom.
8. A trip to Italy.
9. A trip to Hugh Hefner's Playboy Mansion.
10. A gift from the Frederick's of Hollywood catalogue.

AFRICAN ASTROLOGY SYMBOL:

The Baby (November 4th – December 3th)

Body Type: Pudgy, youthful, vital and strong.

Personality Traits: Childlike, socially enthusiastic, good spirit, physically attractive, and entertaining.

Most Romantic Gift: A star on the Hollywood Walk Of Fame.

Winter

LOVE AND ROMANCE IN THE WINTER

Just because there is a chill in the air and a nip in the breeze, doesn't mean the heart must also grow cold. Outside you may see gray skies, snow-blanketed meadows, stark, barren trees and desolate, icy streams. Yet the real romantic knows that while nature sleeps and restores itself, there is no better time to turn up the heat on a love relationship. Use this "cuddle-up" time wisely and by spring you will find your love is in full bloom. Let these suggestions inspire you to make your winter a wonderland of passion and romance!

MONDAY–FRIDAY AROMATHERAPY

Sunday

Relaxation: Chamomile

Chamomile's greatest quality is its ability to soothe. Use this essential oil to make the world right again.

Monday

Clarity: Juniper

Juniper causes great expansion of the mind, body and soul.

Tuesday
Balance: Sandalwood

Sandalwood reconnects lovers with their personal power and sense of attractiveness, making love a more connected and richer experience.

Wednesday
Healing: Ginger

Ginger has wonderful healing qualities and has also been known to enhance memory. Ginger brings warmth and opening to your body and soul.

Thursday
Rejuvenation: Benzoin

This herb specializes in generating heat through the body, mind, and spirit. Helps to get all systems going.

Friday
Passion: Rose

A shameless aphrodisiac that can get anyone in the mood for love, rose oil also is known for potent healing powers that inspire the user with visions of beauty and love.

Saturday
Play: Tangerine

Tangerine will help open you to new, fresh perspectives. It will put the smiles back on your faces and make you feel like "summer" inside and out.

WINTER ACTIVITIES

The Great Outdoors

There may be ice on the ground beneath your feet, but you needn't let your romance slip away. Here are some ways to get outside and make your frosty world a playground for love!

1. Snow Lovers

Do you remember when you were a child and you couldn't wait for there to be enough snow on the ground to build a snowman? Even though you are now a "serious adult," you can relive that fun experience. Ask your lover about his memories of snowman building, and you will discover that this is a winter ritual you both deeply miss.

Go into your closets and collect your most interesting personal items of clothing. For the daring who don't mind shocking the neighbors, it could be a sexy silk teddy or a pair of colorful boxers! After you've collected your garments (go ahead—be outrageous!), head on out to the yard and together build two "snow lovers," one man and one woman. Be really inventive—add a wig and a smoking jacket. However you choose to dress them up, you and your lover will have a great time before your creations melt into one big puddle of love.

2. Gone To The Dogs

In many wintry locales, cross-country dog sled races are becoming more and more popular. Call your local town hall or fire station to find out if they know people who are training dogs for sled races or guided nature tours. Make arrangements to go on an evening dog sled ride through the woods or an open field. It is best to go at night, if possible, because you will be able to notice things in

the stars and in the sky that you may never have noticed before. The calm, cold silence of a winter's night has been known to induce secret snuggling under your parkas. Stop for quick glass of sherry as the pups frolic around in the snow. This night out will clear your heads with crisp fresh air and fill your hearts with natural joy.

3. If All the Dogs Are Gone, Then Try a Horse, of Course

If you can't find a dog sled ride in your area, then try an old fashioned horse and carriage ride around your local park. There are many ornate, big, old, hansom cabs available from stables and farms, or at parks in big cities, just waiting to take you and your lover off on a ride for romance. From the driver's top hat to the blankets piled high in the back seat, a horse and carriage are designed to transport you and your lover into your own private world.

4. It's Downhill From Here

Another game from the innocence of childhood can become very romantic when you're all grown up. Sledding or tobogganing down an icy hill can be great fun as it brings you closer. Slip your arms around your lover's waist as the two of you slide down a big hill on an old sled or toboggan. Instead of holding onto his ski jacket, slip your hands around his waist, furtively sneaking under his sweater to warm your icy fingers against his warm skin. This will be sure to give you both a thrill as you slide down to the bottom of the hill.

5. Figure It Out

Even the biggest klutz can feel like a prince or princess when you have the right setting and music. Call your local skating rink and see if they offer a partner's figure skating class. Glide across the ice while a European waltz or seductive jazz melody plays in the background. It is said that both partners in a romantic relationship require a good sense of balance in order to be there for each other. With ice skating, you learn to "hold each other up" physically and emotionally, especially if it is a first time for the two of you. If the rink doesn't offer videotaping, bring your own camera, and ask one of the rink attendants to film your lesson for you. Later on that night, you and your lover can curl up with some warm kisses and hot cocoa, while you replay the day's event. Finish the night in a fit of giggles as you watch each other struggle to achieve style and grace, without falling on your face!

6. A Winter Nature Walk

Because most of us tend to hide inside when the temperatures drop, we often miss out on the glories of nature in the winter season. When you and your lover allow yourselves to rediscover the natural process of life that is going on outdoors, you gain a deeper sense of belonging to Mother Earth and the Universe. When the two of you begin to feel a part of something greater than yourselves, your own romantic connection will feel more profound as well. There is nothing more splendid than dispelling the myth that nature sleeps all winter. Watching an anxious deer skip through the bramble across an icy brook, or a snow owl blending into a frost-covered pine tree, you will marvel at the beautiful world in which we live. To participate in a guided nature walk, call your local nature center or park. If you would better enjoy making your natural winter discoveries on your own, then just find a quiet, unspoiled place to wander through the woods.

7. A New Twist on the Classic Tub of Fun

There is nothing more romantic than a dip in a bubbling hot tub under a frosty winter sky. Outdoor hot-tubbing is even more popular than skiing in sexy resorts like Aspen, Vail, Park City, and Snow Mass. Don't even worry about being a star on the slopes. If you are a hit in the hot tub, you'll have even more fun. While some go for sipping champagne and eating strawberries while soaking under the stars, you can try this new twist on an old favorite: while

your partner is soaking, pour some warm baby oil on their head. Slowly let the oil trickle down, but stop it before it reaches their eyes. Gently begin to massage the oil in, seductively working the area around the ears and under the chin. Finish up by lightly running your fingers across their face so it feels like rain water. You can also give each other a really killer foot massage while hot bubbles relax the rest of your bodies. Giving your partner a head massage with warm oil as he sits in a hot tub is a sure-fire way to show him that you are a Goddess of Pleasure!

8. Speed Freaks Read This

While some of us dream of being carried away by a knight in shining armor on a big white horse, there are other people who are real adrenaline junkies. For those who feel the need for speed, there is nothing more romantically exciting than zipping across a wide open field in a snowmobile. Grab on to your honey as you zoom off into the white plateau. Sometimes a little bit of danger is what you need to feel like a "damsel in distress" hanging onto your big, strong hero for dear life. Close your eyes and pretend that you're at a chic, Swiss Alpine resort and your man is a modern-day James Bond. Hold him close as he whisks you away from danger to a secret chalet secluded somewhere in the mountains. If you are the strong-minded type that gets turned off by the "rescue poor little me" fantasy, then don't be afraid to turn the tables. Get in the driver's seat and let your man hang on to you. The "Wonder Woman" thing goes a long away for men who get excited by a powerful woman at the helm of a hot rod, in any type of weather!

9. Snow Graffiti

This simple gesture of love can brighten up anybody's day. Obviously there is nothing fantastically romantic about getting up and going to work in the morning. Even if you have great morning sex, the rush to get out the door and get to the office on time can make most anyone forget about the warm tenderness that went on under the covers. While your lover is in the shower or finishing up his morning coffee, run outside, grab a stick or fallen branch and write your names in the snow, encircled by a big heart. Make sure he can't miss it on his way to the car, bus, or train stop. This is just a reminder of the love you two share. It will put a smile on his face as he goes to face the trials and tribulations of his day. It will also put you in a better mood before you have to meet the demands of your own grueling schedule. Being romantic doesn't always mean making an elaborate gesture or a big public display. Sometimes adding romance to your life just means adding a little something special into your daily routine.

10. Having A Ball

When the cold air is making you and your mate feel a little bit more frisky than usual, what could be better than a good, old fashioned snowball fight? Nothing complicated or high tech about this one, you don't even need to leave your own yard. When your lover least expects it, do the following: pick up a heap of snow, roll it around and pack it into your hands, aim it, and let 'er rip! The more you take each other by surprise, the more fun you will have. The romantic objective of a snowball fight is to restore a sense of playfulness and spontaneity to your relationship. Romance doesn't always have to have a serious, gushy tone to it. One of the most romantic things you can do is to let your partner see the light, silly side of yourself. When you feel safe enough to clown around with the one you love, it adds a whole new dimension of love and trust to the partnership. The one thing you must remember when starting a snowball fight is, if you dish it out, you also must be able to take it!

11. Love Outside

Of course, when it's twenty below, the idea of making love out-doors is not always the most appealing, but consider this scenario. The two of you are coming home from a romantic dinner or a movie and you are about to walk in your front door. He puts the key in the latch, but instead of opening the door, he pushes you up against it and begins to kiss you like you have never been kissed before. It's freezing outside, but the fire in his heart cannot be controlled. The heat of the moment makes you temporarily immune to the freezing weather. It is not until the passion comes to a breathless finish that you realize how cold it is in the winter's night air. Quickly scramble inside to indulge in the comfort of a nice, warm shower.

12. Shovel Shovel

When the ice and snow come tumbling down from the sky, it is the perfect time to get outside and play. While a lot of people hire a neighbor with a snow plow to come and get them out of their icy driveways, let's not forget that shoveling snow from the walkway or driveway can be great fun and good exercise (much better to do on a weekend when you don't have to be worried about being late for work). While you and your honey are clearing out the massive white stuff, you can also have a great time sprinkling and dumping it on each other! You and your lover can make your front yard your own winter playground. Snow shoveling, just like having a snowball fight, helps lovers return to the joy of their carefree childhood days.

The Great Indoors

While playing in the snow can be a heartwarming experience, love and intimacy also have a chance to flourish while you're cuddling by a crackling fire or sharing a romantic bubble bath. As the cold winter winds howl outside your door, it's a great time to create a warm, cozy place to share your thoughts and dreams. These suggestions will help you and your lover discover the serene pleasures of "indoor winter sports."

1. Chocolate Toe Body Painting

We all were born with an artistic side that some of us have not yet discovered. A chilly winter's night is the best time to get in touch with your "hidden Picasso," and what better canvas than your lover's body? However, real paint is not as delightful as the sweet gooeyness of melted dark chocolate. Whether you choose to splurge on a golden box of Godiva, or feel more comfortable with a good ol' bag of Hershey's, you can melt away all the stress of the day and enter into your own world of sweet, romantic bliss.

The first thing to do is lay down some big, fluffy towels, either on your bed or in front of a roaring fire. You may also want to light a chocolate-scented candle. In your microwave or on your stove top, melt the chocolate down to a thick, fudgey liquid. While the chocolate is melting, both of you take off all your clothes and get comfortable on the towels. When the chocolate is well-melted, bring it over to your romantic set-up. Make sure it's not so hot it will burn. Take turns sticking your (clean) toes in the chocolate and painting each other's bodies. When the pan is empty and you two are covered in the sticky sweetness, it is time to clean up! This is the most fun of all. Start licking each other, anywhere that tastes good! Nothing is off limits when chocolate art takes over the heart!

2. The Strip

Normally when you go outside on chilly day, you bundle yourselves up in parkas, sweaters, and scarves from head to toe. The minute you come back inside to a comfortable heated room, start to peel off your clothes layer by layer, until you are wearing next to nothing. A sexy strip down of everyday clothes can turn coming home from work or play into a passionate romantic interlude. And it

doesn't have to be the woman who strips for seduction. Guys can play this game, too. You'll love the response!

- When you leave for work or chores in the morning, make sure you BOTH have one piece of sexy lingerie on underneath your "functional" clothing. You will most likely forget about it during the course of the day, so when you both come home and begin your strip tease, you will rediscover a hidden treat.

- Begin to strip the minute you walk in the door. If one of you usually gets home first, than make sure you leave enough clothes on to make it interesting when your lover arrives. You may want to turn on some vampy "mood" music, though some couples find it more titillating to take it all off quietly.

- Remember, the whole secret to stripping basically boils down to four choice words: teasing, enticement, anticipation, and build up!

- There are two ways to strip: you can do it yourself, or you can each slowly take an article of clothing off each other, one by one. Either way, soon enough you'll see each other standing there in nothing but that delectable little garment you put on earlier that morning.

- For more romantic fun, each of you tie your hands behind your back (one at a time of course) with a silk scarf. Then try to remove your lover's sexy lingerie using only your mouth, tongue, and teeth. You know what happens next!

3. Confession Strip Poker, Gin, Gin Rummy, or Go Fish

For those who like to have a strip tease last all night long, there are many card games that help prolong the romantic process. Strip Poker is an old favorite, but you can use any game you enjoy. The rules of a stripping card game are simple and straightforward: every time you lose a hand, you have to remove one piece of clothing. Some people jack up the stakes a bit by making the "loser" drink a glass of champagne as well. Another suggestion is to add a "confession"—every time you strip, you have to confess a romantic fantasy or something sensual that you would like your lover to do later on. If you're like most lovers, you won't even get to finish the card game!

4. Spa Night

The harsh weather associated with winter can have very drying and dehydrating effects on your skin. Since a baby smooth, moist body makes romance so much more enjoyable, try pampering each other with luscious lotions and cleansing treatments that you would find in an expensive spa.

- **Try giving each other a facial. You can do this with products containing essential oils like eucalyptus and green tea for stimulation, or lavender and chamomile for calming and toning.**

- **If you don't want to spend the money on fancy oils and cleansers, then any off-the-shelf cleanser or even soap and water will do. The secret to giving a romantic facial is not about the products you use—it's about how you apply it! Soothe and wash your lover's face with warm, wet towels and lovingly massage the products into his skin with the tips of your fingers. When you gently caress your lover's face, he might reach up and kiss you right away, even before you get to relaxing the rest of his body!**

- **The next thing you and your lover can do is give each other a manicure and pedicure. You may also want to give each other a warm oil foot massage, after soaking your feet in rose petal water. Peppermint oil works best on hot, tired "tootsies," but baby oil feels just as nice.**

- **After the massage is done, generously slather moisturizing foot lotion on each other and wrap all four of your feet together in a warm towel. Playing "footsie" with slippery, creamy feet can wind up to be a tickling session!**

æ Another spa treatment that you can make romantic is the full body wrap. In an actual spa this is done with a seaweed or mud mask and clear plastic wrap, but the at-home version is much easier. Choose a lively, fragrant body balm or lotion (preferably one with aloe, since it softens the skin), and heat it up in the microwave. Make it as hot as you can stand. Cover yourself and your lover in the lotion, spreading it on from head to toe. Meanwhile, dampen some huge bath towels or bed sheets in warm water. When the towels are ready, wrap yourself and your lover together in the towels and lie down on the bed. Experience the joy of intimacy as your bodies soak up the healing treatment.

æ For the final part of a romantic spa night, get squeaky clean by giving each other a light body scrub. All you need to do this are two natural loofa scrubbers and a mild granulated body cleanser. Hop into an invigorating shower and gently scrub every area of each other's bodies, as the water comes pelting down. This not only promotes physical closeness and a better sense of familiarity with each other's bodies, it also helps your lover feel nurtured. After all, we all like to be "babied" from time to time.

5. Heavenly Hair Care

While you and your lover are on the beauty kick, another romantic thing you may enjoy is styling each other's hair. This is especially fun if one or both of you have really long hair. Throughout the ages, hair has always been viewed as the one of the most seductive attributes of the body. Playing with or decorating your lover's hair can be extremely sensual for both of you. If you are the one with long hair, you may want to let your lover braid it, brush it, or put curlers in it. Perhaps you'll prefer just to have it washed and then blown dry. The really daring can experiment with different colored rinses or put in some permanent streaks with bleach and foil. If you or your lover has really short hair, then a tingling scalp massage might just do the trick. A treat for a sexy bald lover is to heat up some baby oil, trickle it down over his head, and lovingly massage it in. Whether you have a full lion's mane or a stark bald top, when it comes to romance, it is always a good idea to "use your head."

6. Winter Indoor Romance, Now and Zen

While spring is viewed as a time of renewal and rebirth, winter is often considered a time of contemplation and soul searching. Meditating with your lover is a very romantic way to make a soul-to-soul connection. There are many ways to experiment with meditation that are fun and romantic. Find a place in your house that is quiet and free of disturbances. Sit in the traditional cross-legged lotus position or any way that is the most comfortable. You can even lie down. If it helps you to relax and shut out the world, put on some New Age or Classical music. Hold hands and imagine a white light pouring down over your heads, washing through your bodies. Breathe deeply and feel the meditation open you up spiritually to receive many heaven sent gifts of love.

It is believed among both ancient and modern-day mystics that there are seven "Chakra" points or spiritual energy centers in our bodies. By opening up these energy centers with your lover, you are meshing yourselves together on a deep spiritual level.

- **All the two of you need to do is envision a white light moving up your body from your feet and swirling around your legs in a circle. This is called your Root Chakra and it is what keeps you and your lover grounded and connected with the environment.**

- **Now send energy to your Creation Chakra, just below your belly button. Opening up this area can do wonders for your sex life!**

- Now move the white light up your body, circling it around in your solar plexus, your chest, and your throat. The Chakra in your solar plexus area is where you feel emotion. When you and your lover have a "gut reaction" about each other, it usually comes from this Chakra. When you give this area white light energy, you are giving yourselves permission to become more tuned in to each other's feelings and emotions.

- The spiritual energy center in your chest is called the Heart Chakra, where the life-blood of all relationships comes from. When white light flows freely through this area, you are fortifying the very essence of your relationship.

- The energy center in the Throat Chakra is vital to a romantic relationship, because it is the source of all communication between two lovers. The energy in this Chakra expands every time you two say "I love you" to each other. When you do this meditation, you are clearing the way for open communication.

- Now envision the white light moving up to the space between your eyebrows, your "Third Eye." This is the center that connects you with your intuition. You know how you "knew" he/she was the one?

- Finally, move the white light to the top of your head, the energy center that connects you to the Universe. Send the Universe your most secret romantic thoughts and dreams for the future. Doing this meditation is giving your love spiritual support and many blessings.

7. I Bet You Didn't Know

Even when you think you know someone very well, there are always precious little things yet to be discovered. Getting to know your lover's secret nuances are all a part of the mystery of being human. When you and your lover are getting ready for bed, pick up a watch or ring they have just been wearing and hold it in your hand. Quiet your mind and pick up their vibes. There is no right or wrong way to do this, just write down what you think, feel or see. It could be a color, a scene, a name, a feeling, or a word. Ask your lover to pick up a piece of your jewelry or clothing and do the same. When you both are finished, show each other what you have written. Some interesting things may come up and take you both by surprise. Don't worry about finding out something that is meant to stay a secret. When you delve into the psychic realm of love and romance, the Universe only tells you what you need to know.

8. Your Romantic Top Ten List

For those of you who prefer romance on a more earthly plane, you can turn a bleak winter morning into an interesting "lover-discovery" session by creating a Top Ten List. Each of you gets to write down ten romantic things to do that day that you've always dreamed of doing but never had the time. After both your lists are complete you will have twenty new things to do. Pick one, indoor or outdoor, and go to it.

9. Hide & Seek Poetry

Even if you failed every English class in school, when inspired by true love, almost anyone can become a Shakespeare. On a cold winter afternoon, when you and your lover are cuddling in bed or by a fire, take a pad of paper and write a minimum of three poems each. They don't have to be good or rhyme perfectly because nobody is going to see them but the two of you. Besides, when you write from the heart, your romantic message will be absolute perfection to the one who loves you. When you are finished, both of you hide your poems in secret places all around the house. Now you get to have a treasure hunt on an otherwise bleak winter day. Leave a few undiscovered—finding a love poem unexpectedly can put a smile on your lover's face for the rest of the day.

10. Hey, Mr. Postman

When you are in the courting stage of a relationship, nothing is more exciting than getting a love letter in the mail from the object of your desire. Couples who have been together a long time, especially those who live together, shouldn't forget about the time-honored tradition of the love letter. Write your lover a romantic letter and send it to his office or even back to your own home. The excitement of opening it up, not knowing what's inside, is great way to give a romance a fresh start.

11. Re-Do It to Me One More Time

Since most people spend a lot of the winter months indoors, it is a great time to redecorate a room or a whole part of your house. Fixing up the place you live with your lover should not be seen as a chore or as a "have to." Designing and decorating a shared living space can be very romantic because it appeals to your "nesting" instincts. The colors and prints you select, as well as the type of materials and furniture you choose, create the environment that you are going to live and love in. It is important to make your home feel like a sanctuary, so sharing jobs like painting, plastering, and re-tiling should be a labor of love you both can enjoy together. Even a trip to a Home Depot can be seen as a loving gesture if you maintain a romantic attitude.

12. The Language of Love

For those who have a secret desire to have a torrid affair with a forbidden foreigner, but don't want to lose the safety and security of a current love relationship, there is an easy answer to this dilemma! Add a little international flavor to your romance and learn a new language on those winter days when it gets dark so early. You and your lover might pick one of the romance languages like French, Spanish, or Italian or go for something more exotic like Turkish, Hebrew, or Farsi. Your local library or bookstore is bound to have a collection of language tapes, or you can contact the Berlitz language school and order your own set. You don't have to spend the time learning the entire language by heart. Just memorize a few romantic phrases in a variety of languages! You and your lover can whisper sweet nothings to each other during lovemaking or any other time you need a romantic pick-me-up.

13. A Sign of Romantic Times

Another very romantic language to learn is sign language. That way you can subtly tell your lover the romantic thoughts that are on your mind at anytime without anyone else catching on (unless there is a deaf person in the room). You can even make up your own sign language and be sure that you are the only ones to understand the messages of love your hands convey to each other.

14. It's That '70s Thing

For those times when you're stuck indoors, a little bit of retro-romance can take you back to those good old days. Forget the CD player or the DVD. Take a look into your ancient cassette or record collection and pull out the soundtrack to *Saturday Night Fever* or *The Greatest Hits of the '70s*. Once you've got the disco music pumping, take off your clothes, and "boogie down" to the '70s beat. If you don't remember what that means, have your own style of naked dance party. Do the "Hustle" and "The Bump" and have yourselves a great game of naked Twister. If you play by your own romantic rules, you should both win the game!

15. A Blast from the Past

Sharing our personal history with lovers can be a really hysterical way to get closer. Cuddle on the couch with a cup of hot cocoa or a hot toddy, and get out some old high school yearbooks or family albums that will take you and your lover on a romantic trip down memory lane. Be brave and let your lover see the pictures of you

with braces, glasses, or that geeky haircut. If you really do love each other, you'll get a big kick about what you each looked like growing up. Even if you hate your graduation picture or that famous Bat Mitzvah album, your lover will appreciate sharing that part of your life with you through pictures, especially if the two of you did not know each other then.

16. All in the Family

How many times have you heard the expression, "When you marry a man, you marry his family?" Anybody who has been married or living with someone for a long time will tell you how true that saying is. Even if you have already met all of your lover's immediate relatives, you might enjoy tracing each other's family history or doing a family tree. Most of the information you need is available today on the Internet, so if you are stuck indoors during a stormy winter day, you two can explore each other's roots by going online. By "climbing" each other's family tree, you can have fun learning about all the people who helped make your lover the person he is today.

17. Art from the Heart

Romance can blossom even in the midst of winter when your creative juices start flowing. Purchase an inexpensive paint set or drawing pencils and paper and two easels from your local art store. Crayons, magic markers, plain paints, or colored pencils will do. Just make sure that both of you have plenty of paper handy to create many different pictures. Draw or paint the following pictures, but don't show each other until you both finish:

- **A portrait of your lover.**
- **A portrait of your lover as a baby.**
- **A portrait of your lover as a child.**
- **A portrait of your lover as a teenager.**
- **A portrait of your lover doing something they love (like a sport or a hobby).**

- A portrait of your lover going to work.
- A portrait of your lover on vacation.
- A portrait of an animal that best describes your lover.
- A portrait of you and your lover together in a romantic setting.
- A portrait of your lover in the nude.

When you are done painting and drawing, have a private showing. Pretend your home is a chic, avant-garde art gallery. Display the pictures around the living room. Pour yourselves a glass of wine (even cut up some cheese in cubes and serve with grapes) and take a tour of your wonderful works of art!

18. Art from the Heart, Part Two

There are many artistic ways to express your romantic creativity, such as pottery and jewelry making. Pottery is a great idea if you and your lover are not afraid to get your hands dirty. If you want to get really elaborate, you can go to an art studio and take a winter pottery workshop together, or you can just play around at home with some clay. It doesn't matter which you choose, the point is to enjoy working together on one piece of art. Whether you make twin coffee mugs, a big salad bowl, or a vase, every time you see that piece of pottery in your kitchen, you will remember all the fun you enjoyed together.

You can even design your own romantic "walk of fame"—the two of you can make hand and foot prints in some wet clay and sign your names, like they do in Hollywood.

Jewelry making is another lovely way to express your feelings for each other. Make tropical necklaces with Puka shells and some string or American Indian chokers with brightly colored beads. Rope and leather bracelets, plain or beaded, are always very popular with men and women. Even if "diamonds are a girl's best

friend," a "craftsy" looking piece of jewelry made with true love and affection will always be worth a fortune in sentimental value.

19. Rub Each Other the Right Way

Perhaps the most romantic of all indoor sports is giving your lover the gift of a massage. A more effective form of romantic arousal simply does not exist! There are many different types of massage to give each other, and there is no better time to experiment with this type of corporal pleasure than in the dead of winter. Give your lover a simple hand or foot massage, but if you really want to show your love, spend at least an hour doing a full body rub-down.

To heighten the physical pleasure of a massage, trickle warm baby oil on your lover from head to toe or run an ice cube down his back. Tickle all body parts lightly with a feather, a comb, or the tips of your fingers. Some people enjoy a hot stone or hot towel massage, but if you really are in the mood for love, try a body-to-body massage. Have you lover lie naked face down on the bed or floor. Then pour massage oil all over him. Instead of rubbing it in with your hands, lie down naked on top of him and gently rub your body back and forth. At the appropriate moment, turn him over and pour more baby oil all over his front. Once again, lie on top of him and slowly move back and forth. If this does not get your partner in the mood for love, nothing will!

20. When in Doubt, Clean It Out!

Usually, we wait for spring to clean out the closets and get rid of all the old junk we don't really need. However, winter can be a really great time to do this because you have so many days staying inside. To turn a chore that would ordinarily seem like drudgery into a romantic event, try a little reverse psychology! Entrust your lover with the task of cleaning out your side of the closet, while he entrusts you with clearing out his. It is always interesting to see which personal items your lover thinks are important to you and which of his things you think he should throw out. While doing this together, you will learn a lot about each other's likes and dislikes, as well as personal tastes. Although you may not agree on everything that needs to go into the garbage, there will be an old Hawaiian shirt or some ripped designer jeans that will give you both a good laugh or revive some romantic memories of times past.

21. The No-Brainer: Rent a Movie

As boring and old hat as it might seem, some nights nothing beats renting a romantic movie and curling up on the coach with the one you love. It can be especially romantic if the man in the relationship goes to Blockbuster and rents the gushiest, mushiest "date flick" he can find. This shows that he is more in the mood for love than he is for the special effects of the latest Schwartzenegger film. Some no-fail choices are: *Ghost*, *Pretty Woman*, *Sleepless in Seattle*, *When Harry Met Sally*, and of course *Casablanca*. These films were produced to induce romantic cravings in all of us!

OTHER FUN WINTER ACTIVITIES

Do a Romantic Good Deed

If the two of you enjoy a happy romantic relationship, why not spread the love around? Call two single friends you think might hit it off and invite them over for cocktails and hors d'ouevres before the fire on a cold winter's Sunday. After they leave, cuddle on the couch and look at photos of the two of you during your early days together.

You Ought to Be in Pictures

Remember when you were a kid how much fun you had making scrapbooks? Winter is a great time to snap some fun nude shots and make a naughty book! Have your lover take snaps of you posing in sexy lingerie and sitting in the bath surrounded by bubbles. Snap him up working out naked in a home gym, cooking something in the kitchen, or sitting on the hood of his car (in the garage, if it's too cold outside). Also take some pictures of the both of you flashing each other in nothing but big overcoats, hats, scarves, and boots. Later on, make a collage of your pictures and put them in a secret book or paste them up on a big piece of cardboard. Another fun and romantic thing to do is hide the naked pictures in surprising places around the house, to be rediscovered later. Nothing helps beat the winter blahs better than opening the refrigerator or sock drawers to find a sexy snapshot of the one you love.

Roller Derby

Go to your local roller skating rink and put on skates. Hold hands and skate around the ring and pretend you are on your first date, back in high school. You may even want to ask the DJ to dedicate a special romantic song to each other. After a few rounds of "moon lighting" (skating to romantic love songs), share some pizza and Coke at the concession stand. Linger for a long kiss before you pull out of the parking lot, just as you would have done when you were teens.

FANTASIES AND FLIRTATIONS

Because we are inside so much during the cold months, winter is the perfect time to experiment with romantic food fantasies. You don't have to leave your living room to have a romantic international affair. An old cliché says that a way to man's heart is through his stomach. These winter food fantasies involve all five senses, so don't be afraid to see, touch, taste, listen, and feel your way into sheer pleasure.

My Cave or Yours

Pretend you and your lover are primitive cave people who do not speak a discernible language. In order to tell your lover what you want you have to act it out or draw a picture. Jumping around the house, grunting, and howling like an animal is all part of the fun. You and your lover should be either totally naked or in just in your underwear as you play this game of primitive charades. Sit down to eat a meal (anything you like) on the kitchen floor. Have a great time eating the food using only your hands (absolutely no silverware).

Forbidden Fruit

Have a biblical blast by reenacting the story of Adam and Eve. Start out by putting a basket of fruit on the dining room table. Tell your lover to secretly select one piece of fruit to be "the forbidden one." Try to guess which piece of fruit your lover picked. Each time you make a wrong guess, you have to take off a piece of clothing. As soon as you figure out which is the right one, your lover has to take off all of his clothes and feed you the fruit.

The Barbecue in Bed

Well, howdy partner! No need to wait until the weather warms up to have a heartwarming hoedown between the sheets. Just get a big towel and spread it across your covers. Call your local barbecue joint and rustle up some chicken, ribs, beans, corn on the cob, and some nice cold beer. Make sure they send you plenty of plastic bibs. Lay the food out on the bed and get naked, except for some cowboy hats and boots (if you have them) or just wear the plastic bibs. You may want to put on some Garth Brooks, George Straight, the Judds, Trisha Yearwood, the Dixie Chicks, or Willie Nelson for mood music.

Love, International Style

Roman Holiday, Part One

For many centuries, Italy has been noted as one of the most romantic countries in the world. The ancient Romans were famous for their love of the pursuit of pleasure. You and your lover can start pretending that you are Roman lovers living hundreds of years ago. Get out of your normal clothes and wrap individual sheets around you to make a "toga." Decorate your heads with grape leaves or any leaves that are the most convenient for you to get your hands on. Pull the biggest chair you have into the center of your living room. Have your lover sit in the chair and pretend that he is the Emperor of the Roman Empire. Feed him grapes, one by one from the vine. After the last one is gone, put on a racy adult video, and enjoy a "safe" Roman orgy!

Yes Madame, the Butler Did It

Dress up in your best jewelry and an evening gown. Your lover should put on a black tuxedo and stand in the corner in silence, until you give him a command. Lie down on the couch and have your "butler" bring you tea. Then order him to bring sandwiches, pastries, strawberries, and whipped cream, one by one. If you are happy with his service, invite him to join you. Tell him that your jewelry looks dirty and you'd like him to polish it. Then instruct him to gently take your earrings off of you and unhook your necklace. While he's back there, order your servant to nibble on your neck and earlobes and seductively blow in your ear. If he carries out your orders to your satisfaction, show him how much you appreciate his devoted servitude!

Medieval Times

Prepare a feast fit for a King Arthur and his Round Table! Serve up some turkey legs, ham, big hunks of cheese, and fruit. Pour red wine into a big bowl and drink out of it together. Pretend that your lover (King Arthur) has just come home from a big battle and that you are celebrating a victory. You are his "fair maiden" and the prize for winning the victory against the enemy. Put on an ethereal Enya CD and do a little "fairy dance." Finish up your dance by curtsying to the ground. Have him formally escort you into the bedroom for a night of love with your "knight in shining armor."

The French Maid

France has long been considered one of the most romantic countries on earth! The musky wines, pungent cheeses, rich chocolates, haute couture, decadent cuisine, and their general *joie de vivre* make the French people sophisticated experts in the art of romance.

This tried-and-true fantasy with a French accent is guaranteed to have you and your love feeling *magnifique!* Have your lover pack a suitcase with his sexiest silk pajamas or briefs. Pretend that he is checking into the Louis Quartorze suite in a swank Parisian hotel. You are the French maid assigned to make the new guest feel right at home. If you have a real French maid costume left over from Halloween, put it on; if not, find something that looks the part. Just make sure that you have at least one piece of sexy lingerie on underneath. If you have stockings and garter belts, all the better. Unpack his things and help him get into "something more comfortable." Turn down the bed just as a real maid in a hotel would do. You could even put a chocolate on the pillow! Next, it's time to bring your cherished guest some room service! On your best tray, bring in a selection of cheeses, crackers, chocolates, and wine. If you really want to go French gourmet, bring in a bulb of caviar and chilled champagne or heat up some *fois gras* and serve it with Sauternes, a fruity French

dessert wine. If you're lucky, your lover will share these gourmet goodies with his very accommodating French maid. Ask your lover if there is anything you can do to make his stay more enjoyable. Tell him that if he doesn't have his every whim catered to, you will lose your job. Let him call the shots from that point on!

Swiss Dip

Winter in the Swiss Alps creates the picture perfect postcard romance. Internationally famous Swiss ski resorts like Gstaad, Klosters, and San Moritz have long been the backdrop of celebrity and royal romances. Celluloid lovers Elizabeth Taylor and Richard Burton shared many romantic rendezvous in the Alps, as did Prince Andrew when he was first dating Sarah Ferguson. The image of James Bond skiing down the Alps and meeting his lover in a private chalet is a classic winter romantic scene. Turn your own home into your own "James Bond" romantic hideaway. If you don't have a fondue kit, don't panic. Just buy some Swiss or Gruyere Cheese and a few over-sized chocolate bars. Melt the cheese and chocolate in separate pans and keep them warm until you're ready to be romantic. If possible, get a big, roaring fire going. If you have some kind of animal rug, spread it out in front of the fire; if not, spread out a fur or fake fur coat. Pour two glasses of brandy or scotch and place them on the rug. After you've set the stage, you can begin the fun and games. Shut off all the lights in the house and hide in the bathroom or the closet. Your lover should pretend that he is James Bond and use a flashlight to search the house for the "bad guys." (Remember this is supposed to be a secret Alpine chalet.) Instead of finding the enemies, he finds you, an international undercover agent. You and Agent 007 are both relieved to find each other on this cold winter's night. Celebrate together by getting comfortable on the rug in front of the fireplace. Bring out the piping hot pots of chocolate and cheese fondue. Dip bits of bread and strawberries into them and feed each other seductively. Put on the soundtrack from *The World Is Not Enough* or put on the sixties classic, "The Girl From Ipanema." If you want to add some humor to the situation, put on the soundtrack from Mike Myers' hysterical James Bond spoof, *Austin Powers: International Man of Mystery*. Make love like two world-class, sophisticated people of intrigue.

Who Was that Masked Man?

The country of Spain also offers romantic scenarios to act out on a brisk winter's afternoon. Zorro, masked defender of justice, is an heroic character for your lover to portray in the romantic game of love. He needs tight black pants, a black mask and hat, and a sword. Put on some sexy lingerie and have your lover lightly tie you to a chair in the bedroom with some silk scarves. He should gallop through the house until he finds you, helplessly bound to the chair in your sexy lingerie. When he finds you, let him untie you using only his teeth. This should be a terrific beginning to a very sexy evening.

Strip Tango

The Spanish tango has often been called the "dance of love"—a very romantic thing to do around your house when it is chilly outside. It is even more romantic if you strip while you tango. Go to the record store and buy some classic tango music. If you can't find any, try a CD by the Gypsy Kings. You and your lover might enjoy sharing a pitcher of Sangria or red wine before you start the music, just to get you in the mood. Have your lover put one red rose between his teeth as you tango across the floor. Every time there is a pause in the music, take one article of clothing off of each other until you are both totally naked. Keep dancing around until you find yourselves tangoing right into the bedroom!

The Naked Matador

Olé! The bullfight is a very romantic Spanish tradition. It is the ultimate tease and test of wills between man and beast. Decide which one of you is going to be the Matador and which one of you is going to be the bull (you can even take turns if you both need to experience the control). The first thing you two should do is get totally naked. Once again put on some Gypsy Kings or the sexy Spanish music of your choice. Whoever decides to be the Matador should get a long, red sheet or towel and wave it seductively in front of the lover who decides to be the bull. The bull can then make a "charging" noise and run into the sheet, trying to butt into the Matador. The Matador should constantly be trying to escape the charging bull while at the same time inviting its charge by waving the sheet or the towel. You and your lover will find yourselves spinning around the room again and again, until you collapse with passionate laughter.

The Fan Dance

The fan has been a crucial tool in the romantic courting process in many cultures. In the upper class societies of old Spain, if a woman was interested in a man she would lower her fan in front of her eyes and wave it flirtatiously. This was considered a subtle yet very direct come-on. Today, the fan can also be used for fun and flirtation. Go to a novelty shop and get the biggest, most colorful fan you can find. Right before your lover comes home from work, turn off all the lights in the house. Have a Spanish-themed meal prepared and laid out on the dining room table (some great Spanish dishes include *Paella*, *Roz con Pollo*, and Steak *Madeira*). Have a trail of candles leading to the bedroom. Be waiting for your lover, wearing a long, fringed shawl and holding your fan in front of your face. Have seductive Spanish music playing in the background. Using the shawl and the fan, do a very seductive dance for your lover that lets him know how much you want him. This is guaranteed to make him ravish you, before he can even begin to think about the meal!

The Swedish Nurse

Almost every man has had a dream of checking into a hospital and being taking care of by a beautiful Swedish nurse. You don't have to be a naturally statuesque, blonde, blue-eyed creature to indulge your lover in this romantic fantasy. Go to your local costume store and pick up a blonde wig and a nurse's costume. Have your lover lie in bed and pretend that he has just recovered from an accident. Come into the room and introduce yourself as "Helga," just arrived from Sweden. Your first mission is get him back to good health. Take his temperature, feed him some hot chicken soup and tell him it's time for some physical therapy. Get him out of bed and help him do some stretching exercises. As soon as he says that he's feeling better, let him reciprocate by helping you stretch out. Sit on the floor with both your legs spread out so that your feet are touching. Lightly pull each other's arms and legs, until before you know it, you are on top of each other.

A Peasant's Passion

A hearty stew and some good ol' brew can go a long way in the wintertime. Find a recipe for a meaty goulash, hamburger soup, chicken á la king, stuffed cabbage, sausage and sauerkraut, or seafood bouillabaisse. Serve it on top a heaping plate of rice or noodles with an exotic beer from Germany, Poland, or Scandinavia. When you are done feasting, it's time for a little polka! Find a Polish club in your area, or just buy a polka record and do it at home. Learning to polka is easy, fun, and romantic. All you have to do is join hands and follow the music. Remember the polka is a peasant's dance, so you can be as lead-footed as you like!

Venus in Vienna

You can do the same as above in a proper Viennese fashion. Just serve *Weiner schnitzel*, potatoes, and Austrian beer while play traditional waltzing music. Even today in Vienna there are traditional waltzing parties, where men wear wigs and the ladies wear ball gowns with hoop skirts. If you really want to have fun, go to your costume store and see if they have big white wigs. You can either rent a "big ball gown" or put on the most elaborate dress you have. Unlike the peasant polka, the Viennese waltz is a very elegant dance. You and your lover should try to touch only each other's hands as you dance through the house. See how graceful you both can be before you waltz your way into the bedroom to stay!

I Dream of Jeanie

The 1960s hit series *I Dream of Jeanie* was one of the most romantic shows on television. The whole show centered around Barbara Eden's character "Jeanie" doing everything in her magical powers to win the love of her master, "Major Tony Nelson," played by Larry Hagman. Before your lover comes home from work, dress up in some harem pants and a sexy halter-top. If you can, put a veil over your head. Take all the pillows off of the living room couch and bring some in from the bedroom. Arrange the pillows in a circle on the floor. Light a bunch of candles and place them around the room. You may also want to light some incense to create a heady eastern environment. Leave an empty bottle or vase by door, with a note that says "Shake Three Times and Make a Wish." Any type of bottle or vase will do, but if you have a brightly colored funky-looking one, all the better. When your lover comes home, tell him that you are his personal genie and that you have prepared a special night of love for him. Tell him to get comfortable on the pillows. Put on some belly dancing music and do a seductive hip-shaking routine for him. Don't worry if you can't do it exactly right or like a professional. It's the effort and love that counts, not the actual technique. Then feed him an exotic dish like lamb *tangine* or vegetables on *couscous* with plum wine and real mint tea. Use an authentic-looking, big wooden bowl and ladle if you have them, to give that "Casbah" effect. Finish the meal by making him eat figs out of your navel. After dinner, ask your lover to tell you what his three wishes are. Fold your arms together and blink your eyes three times. Promise him that in the next twenty-four hours you will do your best to make them all come true!

A Night in the Jungle

You and your lover can enjoy a romantic indoor safari on even the coldest day of winter. All you need is a few stuffed animals and your camping gear. Get out your tent and sleeping bags and set them up in the living room. Strategically place your stuffed animals around the room (a monkey here, a lion there, etc.). Go to your local record store and get a CD of rainforest sounds or African drumming. While you're there, rent a National Geographic video. Buy the most exotic fruits and vegetables you can find in your grocery store, such as mangos, yucca, plantains, jicima, and Florida avocados. Serve the food in the tent, and enjoy the video and music. You and your lover can pretend that you just came back to camp after a day in the bush and are ripe for a night in the wild!

A Passage to India

India is a mysteriously romantic destination. The Taj Mahal, one of the most famous and ornate palaces in India (and also one of the seven wonders of the world), was originally built as a testament of love from a king to his wife. If you and your lover really want to study

the art of romance, then India has two very special gifts to offer you. The first is the *Kama Sutra*, an Indian book of love, romance, and sex. This is the ultimate guide to pleasure on a mental, physical, emotional, and spiritual level. The second gift is Tantric sex, with different breathing techniques and exercises to control certain muscles. The idea is to hold off having a climax, then prolong the orgasm as long as possible. You can find these books in any bookstore's relationships section, or online. Spend some winter candlelit evenings reading passages from these books with your lover while sipping jasmine tea. Afterwards, treat yourselves to pungent fruit curry, then hit the bedroom and practice what you've read.

THE ROMANTIC WINTER VACATION

In the last section there were suggestions on how to turn your home into a romantic winter wonderland. However, winter is also a terrific time to take a lovestruck vacation, planned just for two. Below is a list of some of the world's most sensual hideaways, with something to fit every budget. So pack your lover's bags and call your travel agent. Get ready for a winter trip of a lifetime.

Cold Weather Winter Getaways

1. Colorado

For a tranquil, low-key Rocky Mountain high, slip off to the Wyndham Peaks Resort and Golden Door Spa in Vail, the Inn at Lost Creek in Telluride, or the Lodge and Spa at Cordillera in Edwards. These places offer great skiing in a relaxed, romantic atmosphere.

2. Aspen, Colorado

Think of Aspen as "Hollywood on Ice." Because all of Hollywood hits the slopes during the wintertime, Aspen, Colorado, has become the most glamorous winter resort area in the country. If you and your lover want to hobnob with celebrities, you'll find them canoodling in the Little Nell, the Hotel Jerome, and the Aspen St. Regis, among many exclusive shops, gourmet restaurants, and swanky night clubs.

3. Vermont

On the East Coast, the state of Vermont also offers great skiing, romantic little inns, not to mention the home of Ben and Jerry's (St. Alban's Farm, read the label!) These are some of Vermont's most deluxe winter escapes: the Inn at Essex in Essex, the Equinox in Manchester Village, and Topnotch at Stowe Resort and Spa, Stowe.

4. Oh! Canada

Canada probably has the most the romantic winter getaways on the North American continent, including European castle-like resorts surrounded by breathtaking mountains. For a truly majestic experience, visit the Fairmont Banff Springs in Banff, the Rimrock Resort Hotel in Banff, the Fairmont Chateau Lake Louise in Lake Louise, the Fairmont Jasper Park Lodge in Jasper, the Fairmont Hotel Macdonald in Edmonton, the Fairmont Le Chateau Frontenac in Quebec (called "Quebec's Fabled Chateau"), and the Fairmont Algonquin in St. Andrews.

5. The Swiss Alps

If you're ready for an Alpine journey, join the jet-set and European royalty for a visit to Switzerland's most time-honored romantic getaways. These "grand dames" hotels set the stage for romances of the rich and famous. Take a diamond-studded trip to the Palace Hotel, in Gstaad, or the infamous Badrutt's Palace, in St. Moritz, to see how the other half lives and loves. If you still want the romantic, old world European experience but can't deal with the

Alpine altitudes, check into the Hotel Goldener Hirsch or the Hotel Sacher, both in Salzburg, Austria. You and your lover will leave here with wonderful memories and a killer recipe for strudel!

6. Iceland

One very romantic country that is finally getting the attention of the hip, fashionable set is Iceland. Just a five-hour trip from America's east coast, Iceland offers unparalleled natural beauty to the romantic vacationer. Take a midnight dip in blue-ice hot springs or a ride through the frosted mountains on an Icelandic pony, then enjoy some wild nightlife in the Reykjavik dance parties that don't stop till dawn.

7. The Chocolate Factory

If you can't think of romance without dreaming of chocolate, here's some fantastic news. The fine folk at the Hershey's chocolate factory in Hershey, Pennsylvania, have opened a hotel, spa, and resort right around the corner. At Hershey's Hotel and Spa in neighboring Harrisburg, you and your lover can indulge in decadent spa treatments that include chocolate bubble baths, chocolate mud wraps, and facials. Ask about their special Valentine's Day package weekends.

8. Jolly Good Show

If you and your lover are hearty souls who enjoy a winter's walk along a wind-swept cliff, then the seaside spot of Cornwall, England, is just the place. Walk hand in hand as the Atlantic Ocean crashes below you. Later that night, cuddle up with Shepherd's pie and a pint of England's finest ale at any of the numerous cozy pubs along the High Street. A night in an old English inn will make your trip all the more romantic.

9. Is That You, Santa?

If you and your lover are up for the ultimate in adventure travel, take a trip to the North Pole. Spend a week in Igloo, ice fishing, and rubbing noses with the local Eskimos. Take a guided wildlife tour to spot penguins, seals, and polar bears, or go glacier walking. Or, closer to home (relatively speaking), take a walk around Glacier Bay National Park in Alaska, where you can see ice-blue icebergs, watch the glacier advance, and take a sweet day cruise through spectacular scenery.

10. Ohm

For lovers who want to breathe what has been scientifically proven to be the cleanest air in the world at 14,000 feet above sea level, go on a five-day mystical tour of Tibet. Get in touch with your spiritual side as you and your lover visit the ancient temples and ruins starting in the capital city of Lhasa. Cleanse body and soul by enjoying the local delicacy, a Szechwan hot pot.

Warm Weather Winter Getaways

1. The Breakers Hotel, Palm Beach, Florida

When you visit this magnificent palace by the sea, you and your lover will feel transported into a romantic fairy tale of timeless elegance. Go for a whirl in the magical hand-painted ballrooms, spend an afternoon being pampered in the spa, and end the day with a private meal for two, served to you on your oceanfront verandah.

2. Fisher Island Resort and Spa, Fisher Island, Florida

After you touch down at the Miami Airport, a discreet limo will pick you up and whisk you off to a private ferry. There is no other way to get to this resort except aboard the little boat that separates Fisher Island from the rest of the world. When you arrive on the island after a ten minute journey, you almost expect Mr. Rourke and Tatoo from *Fantasy Island* to be waiting to greet you. Instead, you'll be ushered into your private bungalow within walking

distance of the yacht-filled marina and pearly white beaches. Celebrities like Oprah Winfrey, Sophia Loren, Madonna, and Rosie O'Donnell are regular guests. When you and lover crave a secluded retreat with all the modern conveniences known to mankind, Fisher Island is the perfect answer.

3. Las Brisas Resort, Acapulco, Mexico

Hidden high in the hills above the Atlantic Ocean, on the outskirts of downtown Acapulco, sits Las Brisas, Mexico's gift to lovers of the world. Upon checking in, each guest is escorted to their own private villa equipped with a private pool. There are no televisions or radios in the room, so this resort is really for lovers who want to get away from it all. Each morning, fresh flowers are left floating in your pool and freshly baked, warm croissants are served for you to enjoy. You are even given your own pink golf cart to get down to the La Concha Beach Club. Las Brisas is truly a place that overflows with Latin love.

4. The Maruba Resort and Jungle Spa, Maskall Village, Belize

This modern jungle hideaway is perfect for lovers who prefer to be pampered in a "neo-primitive" environment. This spa offers couples' spa treatments, and cuisine with Mayan, African, and Creole influences. You and your lover can enjoy the relaxing procedures and innovative food by a candlelit waterfall or in the privacy of your own thatched roof pavilion. All the massage oils and body products are made with secret jungle ingredients that cannot be found anywhere else in the world. For lovers who want an authentic tropical rain forest experience, The Maruba Resort can't be beat.

5. Chiva Som International Health Resort, Hua Hin, Thailand

At this luscious Southeast Asian retreat, the two of you will discover more about the mysteries of Asia. You and your lover can enjoy a little "King and I" role play as you dance together on a silky beach under a moonlit sky. This exotic getaway also offers many spa treatments and a selection of healthy and inviting Thai cuisine. You will never be able to duplicate this romantic, ethereal holiday.

6. Mandarin Oriental Ananda, The Himalayas, Uttaranchal, India

For those lovers who want a romantic vacation for the mind, body, and soul, this Indian retreat has it all. Not only does it offer daily classes in yoga, meditation, hydrotherapy, and breathing techniques, it also offers an Ayurvedic nutritional analysis with doctors who specialize in Eastern Medicine. If you and your lover are interested in really getting in tune with yourselves and each other, a trip to this Indian paradise will give you a unique sense of all-over renewal.

7. The Mana Lani Bay Hotel and Bungalows, Kohala Coast, Hawaii

Allow yourselves to get lost in this tropical island retreat. Surrounded by lush tropical gardens, historic fish ponds, and ancient lava flows, this resort is the ultimate Hawaiian romantic vacation stop. Let the on-call, private butlers bring you a tropical drink served in a coconut or enjoy a traditional Hawaiian luau on the beach. You and your lover will feel a million miles away from the hustle and bustle of daily life.

8. The Ocean Club, Paradise Island, Bahamas

You and your lover will feel as though you are on your own Bahamian Colonial estate when you stay at this exclusive resort. Enjoy the gourmet delights of internationally famous chef Jean Georges Vongerichten at the oceanside Dune's restaurant. Mingle with celebrity guests or keep to yourselves at this exclusive Caribbean romantic jewel.

9. The Cotton House, Mustique, St. Vincent, West Indies

A long-time favorite escape of Mick Jagger and the British royal

family, the island of Mustique is a sophisticated yet carefree resort. There is only one full service hotel on the island. Lovers will find the Cotton House to be an intimate sanctuary that caters to your every whim. There is even a special "pillow menu" to ensure a good night's sleep or to help set the mood for more amore!

10. Amankila, Manggis, Bali

Amankila is situated on the beach, in the bountiful rice fields of Bali. This gorgeous resort offers romantic Balinese dancing lessons and tours of the Raja's final home and two water palaces. You and your lover will stay in a thatched-roof suite, and enjoy Indonesian barbecues in a coconut grove. Although Bali is about a twenty-hour trip from most parts of the United States, this ideal romantic spot is well worth the journey.

December

Christmas (December 25th)

This is the big one! Perhaps the most festive time of the whole year, the Christmas season (which seems to begin the day after Thanksgiving and end around Dec 28th) is a perfect time to fill each day with romance. Things at work slow down and people are in a mood to celebrate. At the same time, the Christmas season can be extremely hectic while you juggle your everyday responsibilities with parties, shopping, decorating, and preparing. In the midst of all the Christmas havoc, it is the little romantic things you do that make a big difference in your love life. Spoil your lover with these little romantic treats during the busiest time of the year.

1. The Candy Cane Countdown

On the day after Thanksgiving, go to the store and buy enough candy canes for each day until Christmas. Also buy little yellow "post-it" notes to stick onto the candy canes. Every morning leave your lover a candy cane with a "post-it" note counting down how many days you have left until Dec 25th. Make sure you leave the candy cane in a place your sweetheart will see it and write "I Love You" on the "post-it".

2. The Build-Up

If you've bought your lover a special gift this year—like an engagement ring or something that you know your true love has always wanted, intensify the surprise by dropping little hints two or three weeks before the big day. For example, if you bought your lover a new DVD player, you may want to leave some new DVDs in the car or somewhere in the house where he or she normally goes. If you don't want to be too obvious, leave clues around the house about favorite music or movies. Your lover will know that something great is coming but won't be able to guess what it is!

3. Hang in There

If your lover is having a particularly crazy time trying to fit everything in around the holiday season, show your appreciation. Buy a little "pick me up" like some bath salts or even an afternoon at a day spa. You can also cook a special meal or have a bubble bath and champagne ready at the end of the day. To score big brownie points, hire a "Christmas Angel," an assistant-for-a-day who can help get everything done.

4. Buying the Tree

Buying a Christmas tree is a wonderfully romantic ritual for couples. Make sure you get the right one because you are going to be living with it for weeks. If you live in an area where you can go chop down your own Christmas tree, this will add a warm and romantic dimension to what has lately become a very manufactured holiday.

5. Deck the Halls

Trimming the tree and putting up the tacky Christmas décor can also be very romantic. While you are hanging lights and sipping eggnog, share stories and childhood memories about what you like and dislike most about Christmas. Make your own meaningful romantic ornaments to hang on the tree. Something as simple as cardboard, chocolate, or gingerbread angels that say "I Love You," or more ornate figurines, will symbolize your love. Make a romantic star with both your names inside a big heart for the top of your tree. However you decorate your home and tree, make the Christmas season a testament to the love you share all year long.

6. The Christmas Wish List

Write down all the romantic things that you wish your lover would do for you on little slips of paper and put them in a box or jar. Have him do the same in a separate box or jar. On Christmas Day, shake up each other's boxes (or jars) and then pick one. Whatever it says on the paper you select is what you have to do for each other. To really be romantic, you may even want to start this on the day after Thanksgiving so that you and your lover can enjoy a month of romantic treats.

7. Couple Caroling

Are you and your lover frustrated singers? Take advantage of the Christmas season to be the stars of your own show and go caroling around the neighborhood. Don't wait for a group to get together, just lock arms with your love and go from house to house, spreading love and good cheer. To dispel shyness, have a big glass of eggnog or sherry before making the rounds.

8. Santa Claus Is Coming to Town

Indulge in a Christmas role-play adventure that's more of a romantic tradition than *It's A Wonderful Life*. Dress your lover up in a Santa suit and sit in his lap in a big chair. Take turns doing this—every man deserves a chance to tell Santa his secrets. When it is your turn to be Santa, ask your lover if he has been naughty or nice. Hopefully, his answer will be "naughty." Ask him to tell "Santa" all the naughty things he has done or thought about doing all year long. When it is your turn to sit in Santa's lap, do the same. After a few "naughty" confessions, crawl underneath that white beard and red suit. Then give Santa a treat he will enjoy much more than milk and cookies! Ho! Ho! Ho!

9. Feed the Reindeer

During the holiday season, your local zoo or Christmas shop may have reindeer on display. When you arrive, ask for the corn or pellets available for feeding. There is nothing more lovely at Christmas than staring into the big brown eyes of a fawn or doe, or admiring the antlers of a powerful buck. You and your lover will enjoy the calm and gentleness of such an elegant creature. It will take your mind off of the hustle and bustle of this demanding holiday.

10. Silent Night

In the story of Christmas, the Three Kings found baby Jesus' manger by following the North Star. At midnight on Christmas Eve, go outside with your lover and look up at the sky. Find the constellations, or better yet, a shooting star. Take turns making a special romantic wish on a star you select. You can even give your star a name in honor of your love. (Some museums and observatories have programs for "adopting" stars. You make a contribution to the institution and you get to name a star. What a romantic gesture!) Tell your lover your Christmas wish or keep it to yourself and see if it comes true!

11. Midnight Mass

A great way for you and your lover to withdraw from the hustle and bustle of the holiday rush is to go to Midnight Mass together. You don't have to be Catholic to enjoy the glory and pageantry of this glorious service and connect with something spiritually significant. Midnight Mass is sometimes held outdoors, which makes the ceremony all the more beautiful. The spiritual message of Christmas for peace and love to all mankind can be appreciated by people of all religions during this time of year.

Chanukah (varies, though always in December)

This Jewish Holiday, which takes place in December, is a wonderful time for romance because it lasts for eight nights. That means you get eight chances to express your love! Each night of Chanukah, you and your lover light another candle on the menorah (a candelabra with eight candles and one in the middle for lighting) and exchange a gift. Belle Barth, a famous Catskills comedienne in the 1960s, used to say

"When you're in love the whole world's Jewish." Now, you don't even have to be Jewish to enjoy these eight nights of excitement. Here are some ways to fill your Chanukah nights with romantic excitement. So take a Yenta's (match-maker) advice…go on baby, live a little!

1. On the First Night—Tradition!

The first night of Chanukah can be especially romantic because it is when you welcome this joyous holiday together. Menorahs are made in every style, so spend time selecting one that fits your unique tastes. Just as the sun is setting, put the menorah on a special table which you have covered with a white tablecloth. Put your hand over your lover's hand and together pick up the middle candle to light the first candle of Chanukah. After the candle-lighting ceremony, it's time to exchange the first gifts. You may choose to open the "big gift" on the first night, save it for the last day, or give your lover a succession of little, meaningful gifts along the way.

2. Gelt Without Guilt

The Yiddish word for money is "gelt." During the Chanukah season, many candy manufacturers make chocolate coins wrapped in gold foil packaged in little net bags. These festive little bags are traditionally known as "Chanukah gelt". On the second night of Chanukah give your lover a bag of Chanukah gelt and light the second candle. As you take the chocolate coins out one by one, tell your lover what you would buy if each one of those coins were worth one million dollars!

3. The Chanukah Feast

On the last night of Chanukah, say goodbye to the festival of lights with a traditional feast. You and your lover can enjoy preparing a five-course meal filled with Chanukah treats such as: Challah (egg twist bread), Gefilte fish (fish paté), chicken soup with matzoh balls (dumplings), brisket of beef, potato kugel (pudding), and a chocolate

or honey cake for dessert. If neither of you is a great cook, call a deli and ask them to deliver a sumptuous Chanukah dinner for two.

New Year's Eve

To make sure that your lover knows how much you are looking forward to sharing another love-filled year, make this New Year's Eve a milestone in your romance. Here are some ways to ring in the New Year with a romantic tone!

1. Float Your Boat

Many charter boat companies offer romantic New Year's Eve cruises with dinner, champagne, party favors, and music. While you sail around the island of Manhattan or Key Biscayne, or lull your way down the old Mississippi River, being afloat on New Year's Eve adds an aura of romance and elegance to this very important First Night.

2. Drop the Ball

For those of you who feel absolutely exhausted after the hubbub of the holiday season, New Year's Eve offers the perfect opportunity to relax and recharge with your sweetie! If you've had your fill of dressing up and running to parties and other festivities, plan a quiet hideaway with the one you love. Send the suit and tie and the party dress to the cleaners. Instead, slip into a pair of fluffy, flannel pajamas and big fuzzy slippers. Open a bottle of champagne and whip out two straws to drink it like an ice cream soda. Turn on the TV and count down with the revelers as the big ball drops in New York City's Times Square. Don't feel obligated to do something extravagant. Staying home and being comfy on the biggest party night of the year shows the world all you two need is love.

3. Have a Ball

If you and your lover don't go out a lot, then New Year's Eve is a perfect time to paint the town. If you've been together a long time, it is easy to take each other for granted. But when you get dressed up in black tie attire, don't be surprised if it renews your physical attraction to each other. Go ahead, buy two tickets to the best party in town, and have yourselves an elegant, romantic evening.

5. For Couples Only

If you know other couples that want to do something fun on New Year's, but don't want to go to a huge "do," host an intimate "couples only" dinner party or New Year's Day brunch. After you eat, ask a partner in each couple to stand up and tell the story of how they met. Then ask the other partner to talk about the most romantic moment in their relationship. Couples can also tell the group one romantic resolution they intend to make for the New Year. All the couples in the room will enjoy hearing their friend's "mushy" love stories. A night like this will certainly put all who participate in the mood for love.

ROMANTIC SIGN

SAGITTARIUS *(November 23rd – December 21st)*
Symbol: The Centaur (a mythical creature who is half man and half horse)
Ruling Planet: Jupiter
Rules: The thighs
Gem Stone: Sapphire
Good Characteristics: self confident, vigorous, loves the sporting life, courageous, does and says what is on her mind, needs to be stimulated all the time, loves freedom and fairness.
Bad Characteristics: quick-tempered, can't follow orders, matures later in life if at all, pushy, greedy, can't stay in one place very long, gets bored easily.

Romantic Catch Phrase: "I love the way you always keep me guessing."

What It Means: "I am trying not to get bored with this relationship."

What It Really Means: "I know it's not easy, but thanks for keeping me interested."

Most Romantic Thing You Can Say to a Sagittarius: "You make our love life seem like one big adventure."

Top Ten Gifts for a Sagittarius:

1. Tickets to an ice hockey match.
2. Tickets to the winter Olympics or any other major winter event.
3. A trip to Switzerland or anywhere they offer serious skiing.
4. A trip to the Andes.
5. Flying lessons.
6. A pass to jump out of an airplane the following spring.
7. An African safari.
8. A trip through the rainforest.
9. A cruise through Alaska.
10. The most up-to-date, cutting edge, and expensive electronic gadget on the market.

AFRICAN ASTROLOGY SYMBOL:

Farm Implements (December 4th – January 3rd)

Body Type: Strong and healthy.

Personality Traits: Lives in abundance, is kind to those less fortunate, a born leader and diplomat, self-confident, honest, and calm.

Favorite Colors: Golden yellows and browns.

Most Romantic Gift: A crown.

How To Win Their Heart Forever: Worship the ground they walk on.

January

New Year's Day (January 1st)

New Year's Day is traditionally a time for resolutions, such as losing weight or exercising more, looking for a better job, etc., etc.... It is also time to make romantic resolutions to enhance your relationship all year long. Make a list with your lover of all the romantic things that you are going to do for each other in the coming year. It is the little extra touches that keep the relationship alive.

- Compliment each other on new outfits or new haircuts.

- Cook a favorite meal once a week.

- Have a "date night" once a week.

- Take turns doing each other's hobbies together once a week.

- Call each other once a day from work just to say "I love you."

- Bring home fresh flowers or candy once a week.

- Make love by candlelight at least once a month.

- Take a Sunday night bath or a shower together.

Martin Luther King Jr. Day (January 21st)

This is a holiday that celebrates one of the greatest social leaders in the history of our country and his contributions to the Civil Rights movement. Do something on this day that celebrates your right to life, liberty, and the pursuit of happiness. March together in a local parade or go to see a lively gospel choir for a meaningful and spiritually uplifting experience.

ROMANTIC SIGN

CAPRICORN *(December 22nd – January 20th)*
Symbol: An animal that is half-deer and half-alligator.
Ruling Planet: Saturn
Rules: The knees
Gem Stone: Jet Stone
Good Characteristics: a true friend, seeks pleasure and fame, collects antiques, organized, persevering, doesn't rush into marriage, life position improves over time, seeks security.
Bad Characteristics: gloomy, never feels secure enough, prone to depression, doesn't take to people right away, can be pessimistic
Romantic Catch Phrase: "I feel very secure in this relationship."
What It Means: "I need to feel secure to stay with you."
What It Really Means: "Thanks for not doing anything that would threaten my sense of security."
Most Romantic Thing You Can Say to a Capricorn: "My rich uncle just left me ten million bucks; you'll never have to worry about anything ever again."

Top Ten Gifts for a Capricorn:
1. A life insurance policy.
2. Exercise equipment with a thirty-day guarantee.
3. Arrange for them to go to a taping of "Antiques Road Show."
4. Take them to the snootiest antique auction in your area (try Christie's, Phillips or Sotheby's).

5. Special lights that prevent seasonal affect disorder.
6. United States Treasury Bills.
7. Paint their bedroom bright yellow.
8. A winter's supply of St. John's Wort.
9. A trip to the area where their favorite type of antiques come from.
10. A guide to celebrity homes.

AFRICAN ASTROLOGY SYMBOL:

A *Stately Tree* (*January 4th – February 3rd*)

Body Type: Sturdy, like a tree.

Personality Traits: Entrepreneurial, hard worker, knowledge gatherer, tolerant, happy, genuinely concerned for others, effective but not too bossy, can laugh at themselves easily.

Most Romantic Gift: Balloons or cotton candy.

Favorite Colors: Soft greens.

How To Win Their Heart Forever: Keep a smile on your face, do a lot of fun things together, and keep telling them that they are capable of anything!

February

Valentine's Day (February 14th)

This is probably the most beloved and hated lover's day of the year. That is because there is so much pressure on a couple to do something romantic! Unnecessary stress can ruin any holiday, let alone the one that is "forcing" you to be Romeo and Juliet! The trick to enjoying a happy, romantic, and carefree Valentine's Day is to be as relaxed as possible. Flowers, a card, a dinner out, jewelry, and candy will always be lovely sentiments, but there are other ways to say "I love you" on the day when Cupid's arrow is zinging. Here are some examples:

1. The Singing Telegram

No matter how much your lover swears up and down that this will be too embarrassing to endure, there is bound to be a romantic thrill when the guy in the Cupid suit shows up at the office. Your lover's coworkers will gather around and giggle with envy. Let the office gossip fly as your lover becomes the star of the show. There will be no doubt in anybody's mind that your partner is the one with the hot love life!

2. A Couple's Massage

Find a spa in your area that gives couples massages. Two massage therapists work on you and your lover simultaneously, helping the two of you relax and unwind. You may find massage therapists who make house calls, so you won't have to go far when the massages are over.

3. Sky Writing

On a clear day, seeing "I love you" written in the sky can be unbelievably romantic. Call a local airport and see if they offer skywriting or sky advertising services. Set a time with the pilot, and call your lover on the phone and casually ask him to step outside or look out the window. Can you imagine the look of surprise and shock on your lover's face when he sees a plane going overhead, flying a banner that says "I Love You (insert your lover's name here). Happy Valentine's Day!" This one is sure to be the talk of the neighborhood!

4. Chef to You

If you are sick and tired of vying for a table at a fancy restaurant on Valentine's Day, then you will love this one. Why not enjoy the ultimate, romantic gourmet experience in the privacy of your own home? There are two easy ways to make the beautiful night happen. Call a local cooking school and tell them that you are willing to be a guinea pig for their Valentine's Day class assignment. Welcome a chef-in-training into your home to serve his latest culinary creations for you and your lover. If money is no object, then call the best restaurant in town and hire the chef to cook a private meal for you and your lover. This is actually more plausible then you would think. In New York City, the most famous chefs are often hired out by the rich and famous to do private parties and important dinners. Just make sure you call the chef of your choice about two months before Valentine's Day so that he can clear his schedule. Remember you can only expect a professional chef to cook the meal. If you want to be served or you want someone to clean up after you, you will have to also hire professional wait staff or a butler for the evening. You can also hire these people from a local restaurant or catering company. You and your lover will delight in turning your Valentine's Day dinner into a romantic gustatory event!

5. Days of Wine and Roses

A wonderful romantic thing to do on Valentine's Day is to go to a wine tasting. Throughout the ages, wine has been a drink for

lovers. Sample wines from France, Italy, Spain, Australia, and the United States. Call a local liquor store to find out if they have any wine tasting events scheduled for Valentine's Day. If not, ask them to arrange a special one for you and your lover. Some posh restaurants in your area might have wine cellars, and they are usually very happy to arrange tours and tastings. Or, make your own wine-tasting event at home. Buy a few bottles from different parts of the world and sample half a glass from each one. Also buy a variety of exotic cheeses, cured meats, smoked fish or caviar to go with the wine. Sampling an international selection of wines will give you and your lover a taste of connoisseurship!

6. Make My Day

If you've decided to make this Valentine's Day one that your lover will never forget, then you definitely want to make it an all-day romantic marathon, surprising your lover with romance all the day long. Here are some ideas:

&ofty; **For the woman or man who works in the office:**

Call the boss the week before and arrange for a day off without your lover's knowledge. When the alarm goes off in the morning, inform him of what you've done, and enjoy an early morning romantic lovemaking session, followed by breakfast in bed! But if he absolutely has to go to work, then make him a special breakfast while he is getting ready. Get in the shower with him and wash every inch of him. Make sure to put a something romantic in his briefcase, like a card that says "Happy Valentine's Day." If your lover drives to work, hide your panties somewhere in the car where he would least expect to find them—stick them in the sun visor or in the glove compartment. Once your lover gets to the office, keep the romance coming all day. Fill the office with flowers or have a gourmet lunch delivered in a picnic basket. If your schedule allows it, pop down to see your lover at lunchtime for a "quickie." If you can't do that, then leave a teasing message on his voice mail about how you plan to delight him later. In the late afternoon, you could send a manicurist or makeup artist to the office to deliver some workplace pampering. At the end of the day, have a new dress or suit delivered to your lover and don't forget to include a pair of shoes. Send a chauffeur to pick your lover up from work in a limo or fancy car complete with a bar, hors d'oeurves, and you! Keep it simple by going to your favorite restaurant or do something special by going somewhere that has a special meaning for the two of you, such as where you went on your first date, or to the theater or the opera. Whether you make a big production, or choose to keep bombarding your lover with little sentiments, an all-day romance can wipe the drudgery out of the workday on Valentine's Day.

For the happy homemaker:

If your lover is a "domestic god or goddess," one of the best treats that you can send them is a "chore angel," or personal assistant, for the day. This person will be responsible for doing all the annoying things your lover must do all day long (don't forget to cover childcare if you have kids). If your lover is normally responsible for cleaning, then hire a cleaning crew to scrub the house from top to bottom while your lover goes out or just lies on the couch and watches television. Nothing could be more romantic than acknowledging that running a home is hard work! You can also send a picnic basket, case of champagne, flowers, candy, a massage therapist, a makeup artist, manicurist, hairdresser, and new outfit to your lover at home, throughout the day. In the evening, go together to the romantic spot of your choice. Someone who normally spends

the day at home or running around will love being catered to, even if it is just for one magical day!

7. Hotel, Motel, Holiday Inn

Whether it's the Presidential suite at the Ritz Carlton or a Motel Six, spending Valentine's Day night in a hotel can be a romantic adventure. Depending on your budget and theme, sleeping under a different roof (even if it's right around the corner) can make you feel as though you were on a mini-vacation. If you choose to splurge and go to an expensive hotel, then by all means take advantage of every little bit of luxury they have to offer. Pretend you and your lover are a billionaire couple spending the night in your own private mansion, or that you are permanent guests at the hotel. Imagine you are a hot celebrity or royal couple hiding out from the paparazzi. You and your lover will want to make the most of this night of decadent indulgence!

8. Sing a Love Song

The serenade is a romantic practice that hardly anyone ever does anymore. Valentine's Day is a perfect time to put your feelings to music. There are a couple of different ways to sing to your sweetie on this romantic day. Hearty souls who don't mind the cold of a February morning can get up a few minutes earlier, go outside, and stand in front of the bedroom window. Be sure to leave your sweetie a note on the alarm clock to look out the window as soon as he or she wakes up (you wouldn't want them to go straight to the bathroom, while you stand outside freezing to death). When you see your lover standing at the window, sing a favorite love song. Don't worry about the neighbors hearing you. They will all be jealous and wish that someone did something that romantic for them! If you can't bear the thought of an early morning frost, then get down on your knees on the bed or floor, and sing your song in the comfort of your warm bedroom. If you have a frog in your throat, you don't have to sing first thing in the morning either. You can do your number at a romantic dinner later on that evening or even in a karaoke bar. You may have been kicked out of the chorus as a kid and the neighborhood cats disappear when you warble a note, but on Valentine's Day, it's the thought that counts. This is a testament of love, not an audition! Nobody expects you to be Frank Sinatra, so just have a good time and croon a passionate love tune!

ROMANTIC SIGN

AQUARIUS (*January 21st – February 18th*)

Symbol: Pouring Water
The Ruling Planet: Saturn
Rules: The ankles
Gem Stone: Kunzite
Good Characteristics: social, shrewd, humane, unselfish, talented, affable, innovative, sympathetic, charming, good-looking, outspoken.
Bad Characteristics: insulting, can't stick to a routine, does weird things, no tolerance, stubborn, can be paranoid, seeks isolation, secretive.
Romantic Catch Phrase: "Let's really go wild and crazy. I'm in the mood to break every rule!"
What It Means: "You won't be bored with me."
What It Really Means: "Thanks for loving me even if I am a little unconventional."
Most Romantic Thing You Can Say to an Aquarius: "You are the most interesting person I've ever met."

Top Ten Gifts for an Aquarius:

1. Tickets to a "Whodunnit?" night.
2. A big birthday party.
3. A tie-dyed sweatshirt.
4. The soundtrack from *La Cage Aux Folles* featuring the song "I Am What I Am," or Sinatra's "I Did It My Way."
5. A signed poster of James Dean or any other famous rebels (with or without a cause).
6. *Romantic Intuition* by Laura Bailey.
7. A membership to a gym with an indoor pool.
8. Ask what their wackiest fantasy is, then make it happen.
9. One really expensive item.
10. A sexy ankle bracelet.

AFRICAN ASTROLOGY SYMBOL:

Precious Metals (February 4th – March 5th)

Body Type: Lithe and limber.

Personality Traits: Witty, quick to catch on, adaptable, mercurial, original, fast-moving, exciting, enthusiastic.

Most Romantic Gift: A race car.

Favorite Colors: Silver, fiery reds and oranges.

How To Win Their Heart Forever: Be completely unpredictable and keep them guessing. Be an interesting mystery.

Love Notes

LOVE NOTES FOR SPRING

1. "Our love is wealth beyond measure" in their wallet.
2. "Your kisses are sweeter than a hot fudge sundae" in the freezer on the ice cream.
3. "You light up my life" by a single burning candle in a darkened room.
4. "You hold the key to my heart" on the house keys.
5. "You may drive a Chevy, but you are the Rolls Royce of lovers!" under the car windshield wiper.
6. "With you there is no looking back—I love you" on the rearview mirror.
7. "Your love feeds my heart and nourishes my soul" in a lunch bag.
8. "Our love is a shoe-in" in the left shoe.
9. "I love you heart and sole" in the right shoe.
10. "Our souls are in perfect harmony" on the piano.
11. "Your birthday suit is my favorite outfit" on the bathroom mirror.
12. "Ashes to ashes, dust to dust, our romance is the perfect combination of love, lust, and trust" in an ashtray.
13. "I could live on our love alone" on the refrigerator.

LOVE NOTES FOR SUMMER

1. "You make my heart *swim* with happiness" in a swimsuit.
2. "I want to wrap myself around you" on a towel.
3. "You are my idea of the perfect midnight snack" in the cold cuts drawer.
4. "Your love melts my heart" in the freezer.
5. "You make love like a rock star" on the radio.
6. "You are my favorite hot rod" on the door of the garage.
7. "I'm so glad we're playing on the same team—want to practice?" in the sports section of the newspaper.
8. "You get my motor running in high gear" on the lawn mower.
9. "I'm drunk with your love" on a six-pack.
10. "I want to whisper secrets and nibble on your ear" on the telephone.
11. "*Sock* it to me, sweetie!" in the sock drawer.
12. "You've got me in your *pocket*" in a shirt pocket.
13. "I'm so jazzed to be with you" on a saxophone.

LOVE NOTES FOR FALL

1. "Our love is an endless symphony" in an envelope with surprise symphony tickets.
2. "Hey, good-looking, you get me cooking!" on the oven.
3. "Your love is absolutely intoxicating" on the bar or wine rack.
4. "You are 100 percent healthy for my heart!" in a cereal box.
5. "Our love *suits* me just fine" on a business suit.
6. "Our love is the music of my life" on the stereo.
7. "Our love is as comfortable and cozy as an old fashioned featherbed" under a pillow.

8. "Let's write our own legend of passion and romance" in a favorite book.

9. "You sing the songs of my heart" on a CD case.

10. "I'll be your passenger on the road of love anytime" on the glove compartment.

11. "Our love is my favorite romantic comedy" on the television.

12. "You *drive* me wild" on the car steering wheel.

13. "I want to travel with you down the highway of life" on the passenger seat.

LOVE NOTES FOR WINTER

1. "Your love is so good for me" in the vitamin bottle.

2. "You and I go together like peanut butter and jelly" on the peanut butter jar.

3. "I'll *hang* on to our love for a lifetime" on an empty coat hanger.

4. "Your voice is music to my ears" on the kitchen radio.

5. "You control my heart—please don't change the channel" on the remote control.

6. "You push the pedal to the metal of passion" on the gas pedal.

7. "You're wearing *my* heart on your sleeve" on a sleeve.

8. "Your love is my only drug" in the medicine cabinet.

9. "Our love fits like a *glove*" in the glove compartment with a romantic picture of the two of you.

10. "You make my life sweeter, beat by beat, note by note" on a drum set.

11. "Our love is a beautiful melody" on the car radio.

12. "Our love is front page news" on the morning paper.

13. "I'm writing your name in my book of love" on a notebook.

Getting to Know You

Some of your lover's most endearing qualities may still be waiting to be discovered. Like on the television show where one member of a couple is questioned while the other one waits off stage, there may be some surprisingly basic things you don't know about your lover's past, their hopes and dreams, their likes and dislikes. Even if you've been married for one hundred years (*especially* if you've been married for one hundred years), these romantic exercises can revitalize your relationship and bring you closer. Make a date with your lover to play with this questionnaire.

Take turns interviewing each other with these questions. Don't feel you need to cover them all at one sitting—let the conversation go where it will. Listen well, and be respectful of the other person's answers. Don't be shy! The more you let each other in, the better your romance will be! When you are finished, you will have a more intimate love and appreciation for each other.

The Lover's Questionnaire

What is your lover's middle name?

What was your lover's nickname growing up? In high school? In college?

What was his favorite pet's name growing up?

What was her best friend's name growing up?

Who did your lover have a crush on in high school?

Where was her first kiss? With whom?

Where did he lose his virginity? With whom?

What food did she hate growing up? What was her favorite? Who made it?

What's your lover's favorite ice cream flavor? Sugar cone or regular cone?

On what sports teams did she play growing up?

Which sports would he like to play now if he had the time?

Who were her heroes growing up?

Who are her heroes now?

What are his parents' names? His grandparents'?

How did her parents meet? Her grandparents?

What is his ethnic origin?

What was his favorite fairy tale or bedtime story when he was a kid?

What was it about that story that was so special to him?

Did she have a favorite stuffed animal as a kid? What was its name?

What was the most defining moment in your lover's life?

What is his earliest memory?

What religion does his family practice?

What are his current spiritual beliefs?

Does he believe in life after death?

Does she think there is life on other planets? Does she believe in UFOs?

What are his thoughts about money?

What does he remember his parents saying about money?

What is the wildest thing she would do for a million dollars?

What would she do if she won the lottery?

What is absolutely the most important value to her in life?

What is something he absolutely cannot live without?

What is his favorite room in the house?

What is something she has always wanted to do, but hasn't gotten around to?

What did she want to grow up to be when she was a child? If she has a different profession now, what happened to change her mind?

What is his favorite band?

What was the best vacation he ever took?

Where would she love to go, but hasn't had a chance to get there yet?

If she could be an animal, what would it be, and why?

Who is your lover's favorite world leader?

What is your lover's favorite holiday?

If she could trade places with someone, who would it be?

What is her favorite movie?

Who is her favorite movie star?

What is her favorite television show?

Who is her favorite television star?

What is his favorite book?

Who is his favorite author?

What is her favorite state to visit? To live in?

If he wasn't [fill in nationality], what country would he like to be from?

If your lover could live anywhere in the world, where would that be?

What is your lover's favorite car?

What car does he think best describes his personality and lovemaking style?

If your lover could visit any other planet which would it be?

If he could change one thing about himself, what would it be?

If your lover could change one thing about you, what would it be?

How many children does she want?

What are his favorite kids' names?

If he could pick a new name for himself, what would it be?

Does she have brothers and sisters? What are their names? Is she close to them?

What are her family values?

What is his idea of the perfect mate?

What is his favorite thing about you?

What is one thing that really bothers her about you?

What kind of clothes does she like you best in?

What kind of clothes does she most enjoy wearing?

What is his wildest sexual fantasy?

What is the most interesting place he has made love?

Who is his favorite model or actor?

Who is her favorite star in the music industry?

What makes her the angriest?

What would he consider unforgivable?

What's the nicest thing he's ever done for someone? How did it make him feel?

What's the nicest thing someone's ever done for her? How did it make her feel?

Where and how would he like to be buried?

What is his biggest regret?

If she could do a part of her life over, what would it be?

What does her dream house look like?

What's his idea of the perfect meal? Where would it take place?

What are two things he always wants to have in the refrigerator?

If she could meet anyone from world history (alive or dead), who would it be?

If he had one week to live, what would he do?

What is his deepest fear?

What is one thing that your lover didn't want you to know, but now feels comfortable enough to tell you?

How has this relationship changed her life?

How have you changed his life? How have you made it better?

The Commitment Ceremony

If you and your lover feel that you've reached a milestone in the intimacy of your romance, but are not quite ready to walk down the aisle, there is something else you can do to proclaim your love for each other. Consider holding a commitment ceremony to celebrate your new level of closeness.

Whether you choose to go all out and have a "mini-wedding" with family and friends, or just keep it between you and your lover, a commitment ceremony can be an incredibly joyous occasion. Make it as formal or casual as you like. The important thing is to acknowledge and honor each other and your unique love relationship. Here are some ideas for designing a commitment ceremony that's irresistibly romantic!

1. Write and exchange your own vows, for example:
   "Tonight we are one mind, one body and soul. I commit my heart to (insert lover's name) for now and forever. I promise to love, honor, and cherish (insert lover's name) with my entire being. If ever he should need me, I will be there."
2. Exchange commitment rings. Wear them on your thumb or any finger except your wedding ring finger.
3. Wear clothing that expresses your unique personalities that you wouldn't wear for your wedding (like a tie-dye dress and sandals).
4. You and you lover each choose a personal item that has special

significance. It can be anything, such as a book, a piece of clothing, or a treasured memento from childhood. Give them into each other's keeping, explaining what it means to you and why you want him to have it.

5. Have a local psychic, massage therapist, or astrologer lead the ceremony.

6. Host a formal "High Tea" after you exchange vows. Wear white gloves and pearls.

7. Rent a swank hotel room and have the concierge lead the ceremony.

8. Go to a fancy restaurant and have the maitre d' lead the ceremony.

9. Go to the Bahamas, Jamaica, or somewhere warm, and hold a ceremony on the beach.

10. Rent a local hall or hotel and invite five hundred of your closest friends and family members.

11. Go to the top of a mountain and proclaim your love out in the wild.

12. Hire a ten-piece band to play for just you and your lover. Dance the night away.

13. Rent out a movie theater. Hold your commitment ceremony there, then have a terrific popcorn fight while your favorite romantic comedy plays in the background.

14. Go to a country inn and have a huge, bountiful breakfast for your friends and family after an early morning ceremony.

15. Rent out a local barn, hire a country band, and hold a "hoe-down" after the big event.

16. Rent a horse and carriage and exchange vows in the back seat.

17. Exchange the rings from expensive cigars.

18. Stand at the edge of the sea or a lake, exchange tokens, then toss them into the water, so you'll always know where they are.

19. Buy the most expensive bottle of wine you can find and toast each other and your love, or drink it together out of a "Commitment Ceremony Goblet."

20. Have home movies of your childhood playing in the background as you perform your ceremony. Play the music that was popular during your childhood and teenage years as the movie rolls.

21. Hold the ceremony on a cruise ship under a starry night sky.

22. Have a bouquet made up of imported exotic flowers. Wear flowers in your hair.

23. Hand-make your clothes for the ceremony.

24. Learn how to say " I love you" in five new languages (try to find unusual ones).

The Romantic Wedding

There is nothing more romantic on this earth than a wedding! No matter what the time of year, there are unlimited opportunities to design a ceremony that will reflect your personalities and ideals. Let the natural beauty of the season serve as a wonderful backdrop or a canvas where you can paint the wedding picture of your dreams. Here are some suggestions on how to create a perfectly romantic wedding.

Spring

- Give your wedding a medieval theme and hold the ceremony outside in the forest under a canopy of leaves.

- Have a single harp playing as you walk down the aisle or during your champagne toast.

- Have a posy-picking picnic with your bridal party the afternoon before the big event.

- Decorate the altar in your church, temple, or mosque with mounds of lilacs and forsythia, and drape garlands of flowers along the aisles.

- Treat your bridal party to makeovers in soft spring colors. Give them wildflowers for their hair.

Summer

- Hold the ceremony outdoors in a vineyard. Many wineries offer their facilities for this purpose.

- ❧ Get married in his hometown and have the engagement party in yours. Plan to have a few days before each to show each other the scenes of your childhood.

- ❧ Travel to a national park and take advantage of spectacular scenery as a backdrop for your wedding. Your guests may be happy to plan their vacations to take advantage of the opportunity.

- ❧ Rent an old English (or Irish or Scottish) castle that has been converted to a hotel and have your own "royal wedding." Have a champagne toast on the cliffs, with the waves crashing below.

- ❧ Have the captain of a naval ship marry you. Use red, white and blue as your colors.

Fall

- ❧ Give your bridesmaids "fall baskets" containing chestnuts, carved pumpkins, nutmeg potpourri, cinnamon and vanilla candles, fresh pine room spray, and anything else that symbolizes the season.

- ❧ Get married on Halloween and have a masquerade ball as your reception.

- ❧ Get married on Thanksgiving and have a "Pilgrim" theme party. Serve foods brought to the feast by the Native Americans. Celebrate the joining of two cultures.

- ❧ Get married in a hot air balloon and admire the foliage as never before.

- ❧ Serve seasonal fall foods like pumpkin and squash soup, beef bourguignon, and warm apple cider.

Winter

❀ Have a black and white wedding, accented with vivid red.

❀ Decorate with the gorgeous red berries and shiny green leaves of holly instead of flowers. Drape doors, mantles, aisles, and tables with fragrant garlands of evergreen.

❀ Release a flock of doves into the air after the preacher announces you man and wife.

❀ Go to the Elvis Chapel in Vegas and just do it!

❀ Wear white and black cashmere instead of satin or silk.

Astrological Compatibility

Take a look at your romantic compatibility by delving into the science of the Zodiac. This traditional astrological compatibility guide can help you celebrate your strengths and support each other through your weaknesses. And remember, no matter what signs you and your lover were born under, you can enjoy a lifetime of love and romance.

Aries: Love Under the Sign of the Ram

The **Aries/Aries** Relationship. These two fiery souls may butt heads sometimes, but they also have a very deep understanding of each other. The secret of success for two Aries mates is to love each other with the passion and intensity that you love yourselves. If you feel the need to fight, remember that you are on the same romantic team. When the two of you can learn to give just a little bit, you will have an exciting romantic relationship.

The **Aries/Taurus** Relationship. An Aries can brighten a Taurus's life by helping him or her stretch their imagination and boundaries of intimacy. This relationship can also be tricky because "the bull" and "the ram" tend to lock horns. It is in both their natures to have their own way and do things in a way that suits them—they can both be very stubborn at times. However, if you're both willing to be open to the other's suggestions, and not force your will every time, these two signs will have a fine romance.

The **Aries/Gemini** Relationship. This relationship has the potential for a lot of fun. When teamed up in a romance, both these signs exhibit their childlike, playful qualities. You two will have a great time dreaming up a grand plan to take over the world. The only challenge that can arise is if you become too reckless, thoughtless, or careless with each other's feelings. The key romantic word here is consideration.

The **Aries/Cancer** Relationship. While the Aries individual tends to forge through life with courage and ambition, Cancer is a more cautious sign. The Aries lover must take into consideration that their Cancer partner might not always be ready to go full speed ahead. On the other hand, the Cancer in the relationship should be careful about slowing the Aries down or holding them back. The secret to this romance is understanding and balance. Sometimes it's best to ride with the wind, and other times it's great to stop and smell the flowers!

The **Aries/Leo** Relationship. You two can have a wonderful romance if you are willing to avoid competing and enjoy basking in each other's glory. Both Aries and Leo love to be at the top of heap. The main thing to watch out for is competing with each other for the spotlight. You will make a much better couple if you realize that the red carpet is long enough for the two of you. This is the key to your happiness and your glamorous future!

The **Aries/Virgo** Relationship. In this love combo you have a pairing of real opposites. The Aries makes decisions based on strong urges and emotions, while the Virgo is practical and calculating. This can be a good match if the Virgo can remember not to be too critical of the Aries' heated personality, and the Aries sometimes allow themselves to be reigned in when they go off on a fiery tangent. With plenty of love and encouragement, you two can support each other through anything.

The **Aries/Libra** Relationship. The great thing about Libra and Aries people is that these two can really learn to complement each other. When the Aries gets passionately irate about something, the Libra reacts with a calmer countenance. The Libra's best bet is to smile, stay afloat, and allow the Aries to let off steam. At first the Aries may scream, "How can you not get upset!" but then realize that the Libra's serenity is a gift. And the Libra's life is enriched by the Aries' passion and energy. At the end of the day, the Ram will lovingly and gratefully retreat into Libra's embrace.

The **Aries/Scorpio** Relationship. Scorpio is the sign that can keep the rambunctious Ram on its toes! Their styles are very different—while the Ram will go gallivanting around, issuing challenges, the Scorpion will sit silently until ready to strike. The Scorpio should realize their tendency to quietly take the upper hand can be extremely unnerving for the upfront Ram. The bottom line in this relationship is that the Ram must be able to trust the Scorpion. If both signs acknowledge, respect, and honor each other's power, they will have a very strong romance.

The **Aries/Sagittarius** Relationship. This is an enthusiastic, high-powered, sometimes over-the-top relationship. The Ram and the Archer could save the whales or anything else they take on, since they both excel at fighting for a cause. These two lovers of life have to be careful that they fight the good fight together and not against each other. Make sure you spend some quiet, intimate times together cementing your relationship, and you'll be ready to take on the world!

The **Aries/Capricorn** Relationship. It is hard for Capricorn not to be envious of Aries' enthusiasm and high spirits, and for Aries to be patient with Capricorn's steady ways. Don't let jealousy of each other weigh down your romance. Capricorn, take pride in the stability you can provide in the relationship, but be willing to lighten up. Aries, you can help Capricorn look for laughter, and you two will find a love that works.

The **Aries/Aquarius** Relationship. This has the makings of a good relationship because both signs enjoy a "devil-may-care" attitude towards life. They are always ready for a party and even more ready to plan for a bright tomorrow. Spontaneity and excitement keeps these two signs in a revved-up, red-hot romance. Enjoy each other, and don't forget to help each other stay grounded.

The **Aries/Pisces** Relationship. At first glance, you would think that the hot-headed Aries would be tempted to push around the people-pleasing Pisces. But consider that Pisces is a water sign, and water can put out fire in one good swoosh! The Aries lover should be careful not to take advantage of the Pisces' good nature. If the Aries can enjoy the Pisces' gentleness and not push too hard, water and fire will exist in harmony!

Taurus: Love Under the Sign of the Bull

The **Taurus/Aries** Relationship. See Aries.

The **Taurus/Taurus** Relationship. Ah, what a sublime, comfy, cozy time these two bulls can have together relaxing in their pen! This combination has the makings of a sensuous, gourmet romance filled with the best of everything! Just make sure to go off to your own plush velvet corners of the bullring when you are experiencing a stubborn streak. The beauty of it is that most of your arguments can be resolved with a vintage bottle of wine, a fine meal, and a hot oil massage.

The **Taurus/Gemini** Relationship. While Bulls might not take kindly to Gemini's flighty, flirtatious ways, they will be enticed by the twins' quick mental adaptability and fun nature. The Bull can act as a real stabilizing force to balance the Gemini's tendency to be all over the place. If the bull can learn not to be threatened by the Gemini's flashing eyes and devilish smile, and the Twins can put up with the bull's possessiveness, they will enjoy an exhilarating romance.

The **Taurus/Cancer** Relationship. Home sweet home! Because the Crab and Bull both love home and family, this combination is a natural winner. They will share a similar value system that will make the romance feel safe as well as passionate. However, when the Crab gets sulky and the Bull is too impatient to deal with it, a bit of discord may arise. No big worries, though. A good snuggle under the covers and comforting hugs will soothe both savage beasts.

The **Taurus/Leo** Relationship. Glory, glory hallelujah! What do you do with two animals that need to be loved and adored twenty-four hours a day? Simple: you make your romance a mutual admiration society. Honor each other's need to be respected and admired. These two robust signs will share a lush palace and get along just fine if they let each other be king for a day.

The **Taurus/Virgo** Relationship. Practically speaking, these two down-to-earth souls are a good romantic match. They both have a straightforward approach to life and they are not going let anyone take advantage of them. Virgo does need to curb their tendency to be hypercritical of their bullish lover. The Taurus will not respond well to the Virgo's constant demand for perfection. If the Virgo can loosen up a bit and the Taurus can learn not to take everything to heart, then these two earth signs will enjoy a satisfying romance.

The **Taurus/Libra** Relationship. Since Libras are so good at remaining diplomatic, they have a good chance of shrugging it off if Taurus acts like a bull in a china shop. But Taurus doesn't have much tolerance for what may appear as indecisiveness. The Bull might feel he needs to start making the decisions. This can work out fine as long as Libra agrees with what Taurus has in mind. A romance can flourish here when Libra learns to stay on top of a bucking steer and "go with the flow."

The **Taurus/Scorpio** Relationship. On a physical level, this relationship has the potential to be hot, hot, hot! However, once these two get out of the bedroom, issues of control and honesty could arise. While the Scorpio tends to be demanding, the Bull is not one to be told what to do. Taurus is straightforward and expects the same of their partner, which may not always be easy for the subtle Scorpio. If these signs can appreciate their sensuous relationship and cut each other some slack in other areas, the opportunities for a sizzling romance are endless.

The **Taurus/Sagittarius** Relationship. The challenge here is one that is basic to the underlying natures of these two signs. While the Taurus wants to be comfortable in a luxurious home, the Sagittarius wants to be off traveling and discovering the world. If you can compromise, you can have the best of both worlds. Sagittarius, agree to stay home for a while and plan your next adventure, and Taurus, agree to accompany the Sagittarius on an exquisite gourmet vacation! Fly the Taurus first class and make sure the hotel has a good restaurant, and the Sag will see that his "homebody" lover is far from boring.

The **Taurus/Capricorn** Relationship. This is one of the steady, sturdy, "meat and potatoes" relationships in the Zodiac. Both signs are dependable and reliable—you could set a stopwatch by these people's habits. Since stability is their romantic secret, they are free to pursue other avenues (such as career) to great success. Their passion may not seem fiery in nature, but it is marked by a smoldering intensity that will endure.

The **Taurus/Aquarius** Relationship. This is a challenging relationship because, while the air sign of Aquarius tends to revel in flights of fancy and exploration, the Taurus's feet remain planted firmly on the ground. Aquarians may feel stifled by the Taurus's need to be steady and unchanging. Aquarians are lovable, crazy geniuses that can't always understand what the fuss is all about. What an opportunity to learn from another human being! If you both keep your minds open, Taurus can be lifted to heights unknown, and Aquarius can revel in sensuous comfort they might otherwise never experience.

The **Taurus/Pisces** Relationship. While the Pisces is lost in a spiritual quest, the Taurus is going over their credit card bills. Strangely enough, this mix of heaven and earth can result in a really satisfying romance that works for both. The Pisces will allow the Taurus to teach him how to function in the real world, while the Taurus is comforted by the fish's gentle spirit. Conflicts could arise when the Pisces wants to take the Bull up to a mountain to meditate. If the Fish can remember and respect the fact that Bulls like their creature comforts, these two will have no problem.

Gemini: *Love Under the Sign of the Twins*

The **Gemini/Aries** Relationship. See Aries.

The **Gemini/Taurus** Relationship. See Taurus.

The **Gemini/Gemini** Relationship. This is a fast-moving, exciting, whirl of a good time. These two people are so busy doing, coming, going, seeing, and being that they don't have much time to slow down and analyze their relationship—and they don't have to. They understand each other's need for freedom and space. Lest they whirl past each other too often without stopping, the double twin combo does need to take time out for each other on occasion, just to hold hands and reconnect.

The **Gemini/Cancer** Relationship. While the basic natures of the Crab and the Twins are very different, they can actually balance each other out very successfully. Recognize and appreciate your differences. While the Gemini needs to be running around, buzzing full speed ahead, the Cancer would rather be focusing on home and family. If the Gemini allows himself to be calmed and comforted by the Cancer and the Cancer relaxes her need to have things under control, these two can happily ride off into the sunset.

The **Gemini/Leo** Relationship. The Twins and the Lion both share the need to show the world that they are at the top of their game. They avoid power struggles with each other because their approaches are so different. The Leo has an inborn, regal, lazy sense of entitlement. The Twins spends their whole life rushing around on the go. These two will always make sure that they enjoy the best of everything in life and in love.

The **Gemini/Virgo** Relationship. This one almost mirrors a parent-child relationship because the Gemini is a kid at heart, and the Virgo is a mature, serious sign. The Virgo who always strives for perfection may have trouble with the Gemini's constant flitting about. Virgo, don't be too critical or expect the Twins to settle down and grow up, something they are not too willing to do. Treat each other with care and respect, and you'll find your love will grow.

The **Gemini/Libra** Relationship. This relationship seems to be pretty happy-go-lucky. The ever-changing Gemini and the easy-going Libra usually appear to be all sunshine and roses. Of course, Libra, who is so used to being able to persuade, may be surprised when Gemini doesn't do as she wants. And Gemini may find it all too easy to drive Libra crazy with his elusiveness. Keep your expectations of each other realistic, and don't succumb to the temptation to seek the upper hand, and you two can enjoy a delightful romance.

The **Gemini/Scorpio** Relationship. The Twins and the Scorpion have potential for a very passionate romance, although there are a few potential pitfalls stemming from their differences. While the Gemini likes to be the outgoing, vivacious life of the party, the sexy but silent Scorpio feels more powerful remaining reserved. Scorpio will be uncomfortable if he doesn't trust Gemini to keep his secrets, and Gemini won't tolerate being controlled by Scorpio. Scorpio must keep in mind how much he enjoys the multi-talented, quick-thinking Gemini. Gemini should be willing to give up a little freedom in order to give Scorpio the comfort level they need. A little work on building trust and appreciation will ensure a great romance for the Twins and the Scorpion.

The **Gemini/Sagittarius** Relationship. As a team, these two high energy, motivated people can inspire each other to do great things. Both signs have very few limitations. What they lack as a couple is grounding. Since there is no calming, stabilizing force here, they can literally blow each other away. The Twins and the Archer should be cautious about getting in each other's way. The secret is to stay committed to living in reality while shooting for the stars.

The **Gemini/Capricorn** Relationship. Since Capricorns love anything having to do with fame, they see the Twins as a constant source of entertainment. This brings great happiness to a relationship.

Gemini is a whimsical air sign and Capricorn is planted firmly on the earth. Like Taurus, a Capricorn may have trouble with the flippant attitude of a Gemini. Look past your surface differences for ways to deepen your love and intimacy. You can have a lot of fun together, and enjoy being a lovely, but different, couple!

The **Gemini/Aquarius** Relationship. Geminis are constantly in motion and have a tendency to dance their way around the truth. While Aquarians love the unconventional and have a high tolerance for change, they are "exact" people and demand tangible results. However, these two lovers can have a fine romance if the Gemini is willing to make an effort to be more straightforward and the Aquarius is willing to relax her almost impossibly high standards.

The **Gemini/Pisces** Relationship. While the Gemini is high-action mover and shaker, the Pisces tends to be more of a quiet soul. This can work both for and against these two lovers. If the Pisces is willing to join their Gemini lover and race with the wind and the Gemini is ready to take the Pisces under their wing, a diversified romance can thrive.

Cancer: Love Under the Sign of the Crab

The **Cancer/Aries** Relationship. See Aries.

The **Cancer/Taurus** Relationship. See Taurus.

The **Cancer/Gemini** Relationship. See Gemini.

The **Cancer/Cancer** Relationship: If these two lovers can come out of their corners, trust each other, and open up with their true feelings, they will find the comfort of a kindred spirit. It takes one Crab to fully understand the emotional needs of another Cancer soul. If the Crabs are in a sulky mood, they can look to each other for sympathy. This match can develop a very nurturing, comforting romance.

The **Cancer/Leo** Relationship. These two can find peace and love if Leo is willing to let the Crab sulk without taking it personally. Lion, remember the moodiness of the gentle Crab doesn't necessarily have to do with you. Crab, come out of hiding and recognize the Lion's need for admiration and attention. Love and support one another, and it's possible for these two widely different signs to thrive in a relationship.

The **Cancer/Virgo** Relationship. The great thing these lovers have going for them is that the relationship starts from the standpoint of peace and serenity. The perfectionist Virgo is immediately soothed and calmed by the gentle Crab, and isn't bothered by her occasional moodiness. The Crab is reassured by the confident Virgo. So, if the Virgo can keep the need for perfection in check and the Crab can remain calm and grounded, these two lovers will enjoy smooth sailing.

The **Cancer/Libra** Relationship. The key to this relationship is a sense of humor. Even though a Libra is basically good-natured and tolerant, a Crab's constant need for love and compassion may be a little hard to handle. A Libra prides himself on being balanced and diplomatic at all times and may wonder why Crab doesn't seem happy. Libra, recognize that Crab needs plenty of reassurance and security. Crab, be sensitive to trying Libra's patience. Focus on keeping a lot of fun in your lives, and Cancer and Libra can laugh their way into eternity.

The **Cancer/Scorpio** Relationship. This is a romance sent from heaven! Although there can be occasional power struggles, in most ways this is a graceful love match. Both signs are great at being supportive of each other, because they are naturally supportive in general. The Cancer also really appreciates the Scorpion's deep sensuality which makes the Crab feel loved and wanted—very important to her sense of security. All you two have to do is be thankful for the ease of the relationship, and don't create any unnecessary complications.

The **Cancer/Sagittarius** Relationship. If a Sagittarius really loves her Cancer mate, she will go the extra mile to make sure the Crab is handled with tender loving care. In this relationship, the Sagittarius lover may not realize how deeply her sharp arrows can hurt the gentle soul of the Crab. The happy, upbeat Sagittarius has to learn tact and sensitivity, and the Cancer partner should recognize that being with Sagittarius can bring much joy into his life.

The **Cancer/Capricorn** Relationship. These two opposites have exactly what the other wants and needs to feel loved and cherished. This romantic relationship works best when the two lovers learn to capitalize on each other's strengths, because they are so different. While the Cancer has a softer, kinder approach to life, the Capricorn tends to be tougher, but stable and dependable. The Crab likes the fact he can lean on and look up to the Capricorn. The Capricorn feels she can relax in the Crab's presence. This makes for a very balanced and energetic romance.

The **Cancer/Aquarius** Relationship. This relationship is a lot more compatible than it looks on the surface. That is because both of these signs are comfortable with changes and unpredictability. Since Aquarius loves the unconventional and outrageous, she isn't at all bothered by the Cancer's changing countenance. The Aquarius doesn't think that the Cancer is too sensitive; rather she likes the fact that the Cancer isn't afraid to show his emotions. At first, the Cancer may be a bit in awe of the brilliant Aquarius. However, as the romance progresses, the Crab will learn to delight in his water-bearing lover.

The **Cancer/Pisces** Relationship. This is a very mellow romance. Because both signs are soft, sweet-natured and amenable, there is not a lot of conflict here. Of course, both Cancer and Pisces can be manipulative in their own ways, but there is not a lot of time and energy in this relationship given to that. The Crab and the Fishes just seem to float along through life, providing support, understanding and reassurance. This is a romance that thrives on healing their feelings.

Leo: Love Under the Sign of the Lion

The **Leo/Aries** Relationship. See Aries.

The **Leo/Taurus** Relationship. See Taurus.

The **Leo/Gemini** Relationship. See Gemini

The **Leo/Cancer** Relationship. See Cancer.

The **Leo/Leo** Relationship. If these two big cats can play nice and learn not to scratch each other's eyes out, then an earthshaking romance will be theirs. Both people in this powerful relationship must take turns being the leader. That is not so simple for two proud lovers who both want to reign over their kingdom. Still, with a lot of love and patience, these two monster kitties can be tamed in the name of romance.

The **Leo/Virgo** Relationship. This is a very majestic, luminous relationship, because the Virgo is comfortable letting the Leo be the king of the jungle. As a matter of fact, the Virgo enjoys being behind the scenes, making sure that everything is running "to perfection" backstage. Both partners will need to keep their critical natures in check at times. Romance hits a high note here when the Leo gets a standing ovation and acknowledges that he couldn't have gotten there without his Virgo.

The **Leo/Libra** Relationship. This romance requires the Leo to really stretch and be open to something else besides being the ruling party. Although it is not really in a Libra's nature to start a fight, it is important to them to weigh both sides of an issue. The Leo may be impatient with this, as they prefer to have their word accepted immediately. If the Lion can be patient and the Libra can learn to make decisions a little more quickly, then these two can enjoy a thought-provoking romance.

The **Leo/Scorpio** Relationship. In this relationship, the Lion has finally met his match. As much as Leo would love to dominate this lover, the Scorpion will stand for no such thing. There is more mutual respect here than power struggle, because Scorpio knows the power of her sting. The Scorpio has no problem putting a collar around the big cat's neck and keeping him on a tight leash. Even though the lion never loses his sense of regal pride, Leo automatically becomes much more of a "benevolent despot" when romancing a spicy Scorpion.

The **Leo/Sagittarius** Relationship. There is a good dose of healthy competition going on here, day in and day out. In fact, the Lion and the Archer can create the Olympics of romantic relationships. Just be sure to appreciate the vitality in the relationship and give up the battle long enough to kiss each other good night.

The **Leo/Capricorn** Relationship. Since Capricorn loves fame, wealth, and notoriety, being with the King of the Jungle is quite a treat. The Lion will find that the stubborn Goat is not easy to dominate. However, Capricorn so admires Leo's aura of glamour, she is usually willing to be accommodating. That works for the Leo, and everybody's romantic dreams are fulfilled.

The **Leo/Aquarius** Relationship. Leo is mystified and fascinated by Aquarius' boldness. This creates a very interesting relationship. There is something very seductive to the Lion about Aquarian audacity and bucking of convention. The Leo has the confidence to let the Aquarius bravely push forth into the unknown without looking back. The Aquarius can respect and admire Leo's strength and confidence. Together the Leo and Aquarius can break through boundaries and thrive in a love without limitations.

The **Leo/Pisces** Relationship. For the Pisces that doesn't mind being dominated, this is a perfect love match. In a very subtle instance, it is almost easier for the Pisces to live under the rule of the Lion because it relieves her of the tough decision-making she would just as soon ignore. It can be very liberating for a Pisces to let the Lion rule the roost, and the Lion is very comfortable in this role. The

Pisces can follow her spiritual pursuits knowing that worldly concerns are being taken care of by very competent big paws.

Virgo: Love Under the Sign of the Virgin

The **Virgo/Aries** Relationship. See Aries.

The **Virgo/Taurus** Relationship. See Taurus.

The **Virgo/Gemini** Relationship. See Gemini.

The **Virgo/Cancer** Relationship. See Cancer.

The **Virgo/Leo** Relationship. See Leo.

The **Virgo/Virgo** Relationship. When two Virgos engage in a romance, they need to get clear what's important and what's not, right up front. Two perfectionists struggling with different definitions of what "perfection" really is can drive each other crazy. The good news is, two Virgos with a similar value system and worldview will be able to strive together in one positive direction. They can joyfully kill themselves getting it right all the time, unhampered by the restrictions a less fastidious partner might impose.

The **Virgo/Libra** Relationship. In this romance, the Virgo has to be extra careful not to kill the Libra's exuberance. Virgo, be aware that the Libra may not want to hear your accurate but thorny observations. Let them be, and Libra can go along making life beautiful. Virgo must learn to be grateful for such a colorful and pleasing lover. The Libra should happily go on his merry way, realizing that he can't please everybody all the time.

The **Virgo/Scorpio** Relationship. This relationship can be a real challenge for the Virgo because the hot, passionate Scorpion defies their conservative logic. There is nothing calculated or thought out about this romance at all, and that can really get the Virgo flustered. What a marvelous thing! Being involved with a Scorpio forces the Virgo to live on the edge and let go. This is a real growth situation and a heck of a lot of fun for the Scorpion who loves to seduce the practical Virgin.

The **Virgo/Sagittarius** Relationship. This romance keeps moving forward because the Sagittarius has the great ability to keep the Virgo interested and stimulated. To the perfection-loving Virgo, the fact that the Sagittarius is constantly on the move and exploring the world is absolutely fabulous. The Virgo knows that a romance with a Sagittarius will broaden his horizons and keep him learning new things. The Virgo feels most useful when he can "perfect" all the exciting things that the Sagittarius brings to the relationship.

The **Virgo/Capricorn** Relationship. When a Virgo and a Capricorn team up, you have a couple dedicated to holding up the moral and social fiber of our nation. They will take great joy in supporting their community, forwarding important causes, and pursuing truth and justice. They will have much cause to be proud of one another, and there will be no lack of energy in their romance. This passionate, upstanding duo makes out an outstanding pair!

The **Virgo/Aquarius** Relationship. This relationship is fascinating because the Virgo lives to have everything in life be "just so" and the Aquarius lives to cause total chaos. This romance can stretch the boundaries of both. Virgo and Aquarius will thrive together when they focus on what they can learn from each other, and be proud and tolerant of their differences.

The **Virgo/Pisces** Relationship. This relationship runs best when the Fishes are content and willing to let their lover steer the ship. The Virgo loves to take charge, and as long as the Pisces doesn't rebel, all is romantically well here. Pisces should be careful not to hide her feelings of upset or displeasure from the Virgo. If you're not straightforward, the Virgo doesn't know how to handle it. Keep the channels of communication open and your romance will grow freely.

Libra: Love Under the Sign of Balance

The **Libra/Aries** Relationship. See Aries.

   The **Libra/Taurus** Relationship. See Taurus.

   The **Libra/Gemini** Relationship. See Gemini.

   The **Libra/Cancer** Relationship. See Cancer.

   The **Libra/Leo** Relationship. See Leo.

   The **Libra/Virgo** Relationship. See Virgo.

   The **Libra/Libra** Relationship. This bright, happy, open, communicative relationship is terrific, as long as these two highly intelligent "sparklers" are comfortable with all that sunshine. Sometimes, a rainy day can be great for spending the day in bed and cuddling. The Libra lovers must learn to enjoy the downtime along with the rainbows and firecrackers. If two Libras can accomplish this, then no matter the weather, their romance will be coming up roses.

   The **Libra/Scorpio** Relationship. In this romance, the seductive but settled Scorpion has a positive effect on the energetic, but sometimes scattered Libra. Libra knows that she is in a powerful presence when in a romance with Scorpio. Although the Libra may never fully understand the Scorpion's secrecy and confidence, she can respect and even admire the unique ways of her Scorpion partner. In return, the Scorpion is thoroughly delighted by his lighthearted lover. This is romance filled with respect and good old-fashioned giddiness.

   The **Libra/Sagittarius** Relationship. Although this is a fun-filled, enthusiastic, very successful relationship most of the time, it is not without some bumps along the road. The Sagittarius can be a little too direct and stick an arrow through the Libra's delicate heart. Libra is a sensitive soul who sometimes hides behind a shining smile. The Sagittarius must make it a point not to take this for granted. With a little tact and honesty, these two lovers can have a wonderful time on their mutual quest to live life to the fullest.

The **Libra/Capricorn** Relationship. A Libra lover is born to fly and won't be easy to hold down. At the same time, a Libra can love and appreciate the constant stability that a Capricorn brings to their romance. Recognize and acknowledge that you are very different souls right from the start. If the Capricorn can let himself have a good laugh and the Libra can use that famous diplomacy when necessary, an enjoyable romance will be theirs.

The **Libra/Aquarius** Relationship. Both parties in a Libra/Aquarius relationship are used to being a little unconventional. The Aquarian gets a kick out of being "crazy" in the far-out, rebellious sense of the word. To the Libra, "crazy" means shaving cream fights on Halloween and sack races with the third-graders. The secret for these two is to avoid competing for the spotlight and not try to outdo each other. If Libra and Aquarius want to stay romantically entwined, then they have to realize that there is enough "craziness" to go around in this world.

The **Libra/Pisces** Relationship. This is a very balanced romance because both signs really love each other's softer side. The sensitive Pisces is refreshed by the Libra's bubbly persona and appreciates the Libra's diplomacy. The Libra feels loved and comfortable because he knows that he isn't going to be emotionally torn apart. In this warm, safe romance, both lovers are free to live, breathe, and fantasize to each other's delight.

Scorpio: Love Under the Sign of the Scorpion
The **Scorpio/Aries** Relationship. See Aries.

The **Scorpio/Taurus** Relationship. See Taurus.

The **Scorpio/Gemini** Relationship. See Gemini.

The **Scorpio/Cancer** Relationship. See Cancer.

The **Scorpio/Leo** Relationship. See Leo.

The **Scorpio/Virgo** Relationship. See Virgo.

The **Scorpio/Libra** Relationship. See Libra.

The **Scorpio/Scorpio** Relationship. The double Scorpion relationship is a deeply passionate romance with an intriguing air of mystery. The pitfall for two Scorpions is competitiveness—who can keep the most secrets, who can be the more sexually adventurous, and who is still more attractive to people outside the relationship. Scorpions feel best when they have the upper hand, so loving someone of their own persuasion can be tricky. However, when these two lovers allow themselves to get in sync, it is a sensuous celebration worth everything they put into it.

The **Scorpio/Sagittarius** Relationship. As with any challenging match, the rewards available here are great. Scorpio may wish that Sagittarius would slow down long enough for nice hot bath and a massage. While Sagittarius is attracted to Scorpio's air of mystery, she's not really comfortable with having to guess at the Scorpion's true feelings. When Scorpio is willing to open up some and Sagittarius is willing to curb some of her sharpness, then their romance can be deeply satisfying to both.

The **Scorpio/Capricorn** Relationship. This romance is based on both lovers' desires for respect, trust, and confidence. While both signs tend to feel superior, in this relationship their confidence works in their favor because it allows both of them to feel relaxed and at ease with each other. Not only that, the Capricorn is thrilled by the sexy Scorpion's aura of power and sensuousness. And while Scorpio relates well to Capricorn's settled approach to life, he also enjoy the effect he can have on a normally reserved Capricorn.

The **Scorpio/Aquarius** Relationship. This is a highly-charged romance. The Aquarius' outrageousness doesn't always sit well with the silent Scorpion. The Aquarius doesn't really understand his lover's deep reserve. As with any pairing of opposites, the key is to respect each other's differences. Aquarius can win Scorpio's trust by not making light of the secrets that Scorpio wishes to protect. Scorpio can accept the high-flying Aquarius and be willing to crack her protective shell enough to let her lover in.

The **Scorpio/Pisces** Relationship. This is a heaven-sent relationship with a deeply spiritual connection. For reasons unknown to the outside world, these two lovers are very much in tune to each other's desires and needs. Somehow, instinctively they know how to take care of each other. This doesn't usually involve much talking or discussing. The romantic communication is done on another level. To watch these two is to observe two lovers moving in perfect harmony with each other.

Sagittarius: Love Under the Sign of the Archer

The **Sagittarius/Aries** Relationship. See Aries.

The **Sagittarius/Taurus** Relationship. See Taurus.

The **Sagittarius/Gemini** Relationship. See Gemini.

The **Sagittarius/Cancer** Relationship. See Cancer.

The **Sagittarius/Leo** Relationship. See Leo.

The **Sagittarius/Virgo** Relationship. See Virgo.

The **Sagittarius/Libra** Relationship. See Libra.

The **Sagittarius/Scorpio** Relationship. See Scorpio.

The **Sagittarius/Sagittarius** Relationship. A little kindness and consideration will go a long way in making this relationship work. You would think that because these two lovers are so heavily influenced by Jupiter, their relationship would be filled with endless positive expansion. Unfortunately, the abundance of wanderlust and frankness that characterizes this sign can wreak havoc on the egos of two Sagittarius lovers in a romantic pair. These two can capitalize on their strengths if they keep active, plan a lot of travel together, and keep rubber tips on those arrows when an argument lets them loose. Remember what you love about each other, and enjoy a vigorous romance.

The **Sagittarius/Capricorn** Relationship. Oddly enough, the settled, stable Capricorn is delighted by the flighty Sagittarius. As a matter of fact, Capricorns find a Sagittarius' endless quest for the world's jewels a real plus, attracted as she is to fame and fortune. Capricorn is invigorated by the Archer's enthusiasm and energy. Because the Capricorn is so sharp and well-versed, the Sagittarius doesn't seem to mind a sometimes staid demeanor. Strangely, the Capricorn's bouts of selfishness can be very appealing to the Sagittarius simply because he understands it so well. Therefore these strange bedfellows can have a romance that is as solid as it is spicy.

The **Sagittarius/Aquarius** Relationship. These two freedom-loving signs know no boundaries. A romance between a Sagittarius and an Aquarius is likely to be a spectacular affair marked by brilliance, humor, and mind-blowing accomplishment—if they don't get arrested. When all is said and done, the Sagittarius and the Aquarius will share a legendary love and a life without limitations.

The **Sagittarius/Pisces** Relationship. In this romance, you have one fast-talking, energetic, hard-nosed optimist and one soft-spoken, watery dreamer. Sometimes the strangest combinations work! The good news for the Sagittarius is that they don't have to worry about the Fishes judging them or questioning their haphazard travels. The Pisces is not inclined to quell the Sagittarius' sense of adventure because it is not a sign that has to stay in one place to feel secure. The Pisces will encourage the Sagittarius to stop and think before they speak, which is not a bad thing for a Sagittarius to learn. With a lot of love and mutual respect, this romance can go swimmingly.

Capricorn: Love Under the Sign of the Goat
The **Capricorn/Aries** Relationship. See Aries.

The **Capricorn/Taurus** Relationship. See Taurus.

The **Capricorn/Gemini** Relationship. See Gemini.

The **Capricorn/Cancer** Relationship. See Cancer.

The **Capricorn/Leo** Relationship. See Leo.

The **Capricorn/Virgo** Relationship. See Virgo.

The **Capricorn/Libra** Relationship. See Libra.

The **Capricorn/Scorpio** Relationship. See Scorpio.

The **Capricorn/Sagittarius** Relationship. See Sagittarius.

The **Capricorn/Capricorn** Relationship. Like the antiques that the Capricorn loves to collect, this romance gets better with time. When these two lovers are just starting out in life, it is their natural inclination to do things on the straight and narrow. As they mature, however, their need to "live by the book" loosens up quite a bit. In their later years, the more frivolous, fun-loving side of the Capricorn takes over. In fact, the sooner two Capricorns decide that life is too short to be restricted by Saturn, the party and the romance will really take off.

The **Capricorn/Aquarius** Relationship. It's hard to generalize about a Capricorn/Aquarius relationship. The success of this romance is going to depend upon the tolerance and patience of the individuals. It is instinctive to the Aquarius to shake things up. However, the Capricorn loves everything to be in order and under control. Will the Capricorn be able to smile at the outrageous behavior of the Aquarius? Will the Aquarius be patient and behave himself when they accompany the Capricorn to a town meeting or fundraiser? If both lovers are absolutely committed to each other and willing to do things that don't necessarily come naturally, their romance will thrive despite any astrological differences.

The **Capricorn/Pisces** Relationship. This is a match of opposites that can harmonize beautifully. The Pisces loves the sense of stability and security that the Capricorn provides and in turn, the Capricorn is entranced by the sweetness and light that the Pisces brings to their romance. The Capricorn may even feel inclined to "lighten up" in the presence of a Pisces lover, and the Pisces may find themselves thinking about the down-to-earth pursuits that are dear to the heart of their Capricorn lover. This makes the Capricorn/Pisces romance a miraculous twist of nature, indeed!

Aquarius: Love Under the Sign of the Water Bearer

The **Aquarius/Aries** Relationship. See Aries.

The **Aquarius/Taurus** Relationship. See Taurus.

The **Aquarius/Gemini** Relationship. See Gemini.

The **Aquarius/Cancer** Relationship. See Cancer.

The **Aquarius/Leo** Relationship. See Leo.

The **Aquarius/Virgo** Relationship. See Virgo.

The **Aquarius/Libra** Relationship. See Libra.

The **Aquarius/Scorpio** Relationship. See Scorpio.

The **Aquarius/Sagittarius** Relationship. See Sagittarius.

The **Aquarius/Capricorn** Relationship. See Capricorn.

The **Aquarius/Aquarius** Relationship. Do you remember the kid on your block who had the really freaky parents? This kid's parents were the kind of people who thought a fun day at Disney World was more important than homework and encouraged the child to debate his teacher's point of view. This is exactly what you get when two Aquarians enter into a romantic relationship—a lovely, exciting, irresistible adventure. Friends and family will no doubt be both envious and extremely entertained by this wacky duo. Outsiders will admire or be amazed by the freedom and jubilation that Aquarian lovers experience on a daily basis. They may be a constant source of gossip, but this couple of wild and crazy kids will have the time of their lives.

The **Aquarius/Pisces** Relationship. This is a spiritually-charged merger of mind, body, and soul. The lucky partners in a Pisces/Aquarius romance can rule the world—or at least make a difference while enjoying a highly successful and satisfying life together. When the energy and daring of the Aquarius teams up with the boundless creativity of the idealistic Pisces, magic can happen! There's just no underestimating the power of a Pisces/Aquarius romance.

Pisces: Love Under the Sign of the Fish

The **Pisces/Aries** Relationship. See Aries.

The **Pisces/Taurus** Relationship. See Taurus.

The **Pisces/Gemini** Relationship. See Gemini.

The **Pisces/Cancer** Relationship. See Cancer.

The **Pisces/Leo** Relationship. See Leo.

The **Pisces/Virgo** Relationship. See Virgo.

The **Pisces/Libra** Relationship. See Libra.

The **Pisces/Scorpio** Relationship. See Scorpio.

The **Pisces/Sagittarius** Relationship. See Sagittarius.

The **Pisces/Capricorn** Relationship. See Capricorn.

The **Pisces/Aquarius** Relationship. See Aquarius.

The **Pisces/Pisces** Relationship. Imagine two angels here on earth having a romantic relationship among us wee mortal folk. This pretty much sums up the Pisces/Pisces romance. Not that either lover behaves like an angel all the time. Yet the ever-present theme of this romance is divine serenity. These Fishes give each other unlimited permission to dream and live an ephemeral existence. The only bummer here is that someone is going to have to balance the checkbook!

Romantic Farewell

I hope that you have enjoyed this book and discovered new ways to rejuvenate your romance. No matter whether you've been married for forty years, been living together for four months, or just been seeing each other for four days, the time is always right to make the most of your romance. Every day of every season creates a new opportunity for your love to expand and flourish. May you now know that, be it spring, summer, fall, or winter, each time of year holds a special possibility for you to celebrate your romance with the one you love. Take advantage of all that the changing seasons have to offer.

The most important thing to remember is that romance is like a flame that needs to be constantly fanned to burn brightly! It is up to you and your lover to help that flame grow into a passionate fire that lights up your lives. There is no limit to how much your love can deepen when you make a point to do something romantic every day of the year. So don't forget to buy those roses on the way home from work, call just to say "I love you," hold hands in the movie theater, and tell each other how much you make each other's lives an exciting romantic adventure!

About the Author

Mara Goodman-Davies is a journalist and publicity consultant. She has written on health, food and sex, and fiction. Her "Sex and Food" column appears in *Oui* magazine. She is newly married and lives in New York City.